Southern Living®
Cookbook
Library

The
Canning
& Preserving
Cookbook

Copyright© 1972 Oxmoor House, Inc.
All rights reserved.
Library of Congress Catalog Number: 76–45871
ISBN: 0–8487–0333–2

Cover: Jam of Four Berries (page 86)
Left: Pear Marmalade (page 104)
  Tomato Marmalade (page 104)

contents

Easy Pickled Crab Apples (page 136)
Spiced Fresh Cherries (page 134)
Spiced Orange Wedges (page 20)
Pickled Green Grapes (page 136)

preface

The rich farmlands and temperate climate of the South combine to produce a lengthy growing season with as many as two and sometimes even three crops to harvest. Food preservation is a tradition in the Southland, and women from every state in the region have shared their most treasured recipes with you in this *Canning and Preserving Cookbook.*

In the pages of this cookbook, you'll discover recipes for preserving fruits and juices . . . vegetables . . . meats, poultry, and seafood . . . soup and sauces . . . jams, jellies, and marmalades . . . conserves and preserves . . . and pickles and relishes. There's even a section on how to freeze every kind of food imaginable.

Accompanying these recipes are page after page of the latest information on how to can and preserve foods successfully and safely. Turn through these pages and learn how to plan a garden for later canning and preserving . . . how to estimate quantities of food for canning and preserving . . . how many jars you'll need . . . the correct way to process various foods . . . how to solve canning problems . . . the seasonings to use . . . and much more.

This is a very special book about a very special area of food preparation — canning and preserving. From our kitchens to yours, welcome to the wonderful world of canning and preserving — southern style!

There are three basic methods of canning and preserving: the steam-pressure, water-bath, and open-kettle method. The particular method used depends on the type of food to be processed, as explained more fully below. The steam-pressure method requires special equipment; most kitchens are already equipped with the utensils needed in the other two processes. Of the three methods, perhaps the open-kettle procedure is the fastest. All, however, are equally satisfying and yield home-canned products that you'll be proud of.

Always rely on one of the three methods described below for successful canning and preserving. Avoid shortcut methods. Oven canning is dangerous: when placed in a hot oven, jars may explode and cause damage.

Steam-Pressure Method – The steam-pressure method processes foods under

methods
OF CANNING AND PRESERVING

pressure at a temperature of 240 degrees. A special steam-pressure canner or cooker is required. It supplies the intense heat needed for destruction of bacteria in low-acid foods such as beans, beets, corn, and meats.

A steam-pressure canner consists of a heavy kettle with a rack. It also has a cover that can be clamped or locked down to make the kettle steamtight. The cover is fitted with a safety valve and a vent (or petcock) that can be opened or closed to allow steam to escape or to trap it. Also on the cover is a pressure gauge that indicates pressure during processing.

In the steam-pressure method, the canner is filled with about 2 to 3 inches of water. The canner is then placed on a heat source and the water is heated. As each canning jar is filled, it is placed in the hot water on the canner's rack. Jars should not touch one another so that steam can flow freely around each one during processing.

After the jars are placed on the rack, the canner cover is securely fastened. The vent is left open. For about 10 minutes steam is allowed to escape through the vent for a seven quart canner. This step is called "venting" or "exhausting"; it removes the air from inside the canner. Air left in the canner during processing causes underprocessing of food and consequent food spoilage.

Next the vent is closed and the pressure is permitted to rise. Processing time is counted from the moment the gauge registers the pressure specified in the recipe. Food is processed for the length of time recommended in the recipe.

During the entire process, the pressure is kept constant by regulation of the heat source. Pressure should never be lowered by opening the vent or allowing a cold draft to blow around the canner.

When processing time is completed, the canner is removed from the heat source. It is allowed to cool *naturally*, away from cold drafts. The pressure gauge is permitted to return to 0. Two minutes later, the vent is slowly opened and the cover unfastened.

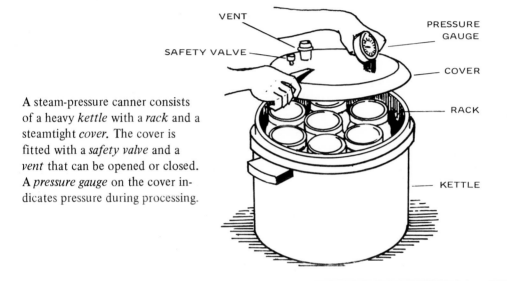

VENT

SAFETY VALVE

PRESSURE GAUGE

COVER

RACK

KETTLE

A steam-pressure canner consists of a heavy *kettle* with a *rack* and a steamtight *cover*. The cover is fitted with a *safety valve* and a *vent* that can be opened or closed. A *pressure gauge* on the cover indicates pressure during processing.

Water-Bath Method — The water-bath method is a way of processing foods in boiling water at a temperature of 212 degrees. Enough heat is supplied by the boiling water to destroy the substances that cause spoilage in acid foods such as fruits, tomatoes, and rhubarb. This method is not recommended for canning low-acid foods that require more intense heat.

A water-bath canner consists simply of a large kettle with a cover and a rack or metal basket. The kettle needs to be about 6 inches deeper than a standard canning jar. The extra space allows for 1 to 2 inches of water over jar tops and for boiling room.

The rack or basket is placed on the bottom of the kettle before processing. Jars rest on it rather than directly on the bottom of the kettle. This permits free water circulation under the jars during processing.

A standard steam-pressure canner can be used in the water-bath method. In this case, the cover of the canner is not fastened down tightly and the vent is left open during processing.

In the water-bath method, the canner is filled half full with water. It is then

7

placed on the stove to allow water to heat. If food is packed into the jars cold or raw, the water is heated until hot, not boiling. If food is packed into the jars precooked and hot, the water is brought to the boiling point. This is the only step in the water-bath method that varies depending on the way the food is packed.

Filled jars, whether raw-packed or hot-packed, are placed in the water on the rack. Jars are spaced apart from one another to permit water to circulate freely around each one. Enough boiling water to cover the tops of the jars 1 to 2 inches is added. The kettle is then covered.

Processing time is counted when the water either (1) comes to a full rolling boil in the case of raw-packed foods, or (2) returns to a full rolling boil in the case of hot-packed foods. Water is kept at a vigorous boil throughout processing. If the water should stop boiling for any reason, additional processing time must be allowed; the process is not started over again. If necessary, more boiling water is added to the canner during processing to keep the water level above the jar tops. Food is processed for the amount of time recommended in a specific recipe. When processing time is up, the canner is removed from the heat source. Then the jars are immediately taken out of the canner.

A water-bath canner consists of a large *kettle,* a *cover,* and a *rack* (or metal basket). The kettle must be several inches deeper than a standard canning jar. The extra space permits the tops of the canning jars to be covered with water during processing and allows for boiling room.

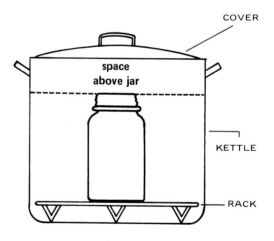

Open-kettle Method — In the open-kettle method, food is cooked in an uncovered kettle. Food is then poured boiling hot into sterilized jars. Each jar is quickly sealed before another one is filled. *Jars are not processed* by either steam pressure or boiling water.

This method is recommended especially for jellies, some jams, conserves, fruit butters, marmalades, and preserves. But to prevent mold from forming it is best to water bath everything but jellies. The open-kettle procedure should also be used only when a storage temperature of 65 degrees or below can be maintained. Hot and humid storage conditions promote speedy spoilage of foods canned by the water-bath method.

Home canning can be one of the most enjoyable experiences you'll ever have. You'll find pleasure in the canning process itself and pride when you view your own home-canned jars of food. To a great extent success in canning depends on proper equipment and handling of equipment, food planning and quality foods, and correct procedure. Here are some helpful hints about equipment, food, and procedure for maximum canning efficiency and success.

Equipment — Before the canning season begins, see what canning supplies you have on hand and check their condition. Then list any additional supplies you will need to buy. Plan to buy them in advance of the canning season when most stores have ample quantities.

Equipment that you must have includes canning jars; jar fittings such as lids,

successful

CANNING AND PRESERVING

metal bands, caps, and rubber rings; and a steam-pressure canner and/or water-bath canner. In addition to these items that you must have for proper equipment, there are common kitchen utensils that will make canning easier for you: a jar lifter, a funnel, a ladle with lip, a sieve, a colander, a food mill, large trays, and sharp knives.

Plan to use only standard preserving jars made especially for home canning. Commercial food jars are usually not strong enough to withstand the pressure or heat that is used in the canning process. Check jars for cracks, nicks, or chips; these imperfections prevent airtight sealing. Discard jars with defects. The JAR ESTIMATE GUIDE on page 11 will help you determine how many jars to have on hand for the quantity of food you plan to can.

If you plan to use metal bands examine them for warping or rusting and throw away unusable bands. When testing the usability of rubber rings, don't stretch them out of shape. Always plan on buying new self-sealing lids; lids should not be used more than once.

Examine your steam-pressure canner or water-bath canner to be sure that it is in perfect condition. All parts of a steam-pressure canner (see pages 6-8) must be clean and in good working order. Wash the kettle of the steam-pressure canner well; wipe the cover with a soapy cloth and then remove soap with a damp cloth. Don't immerse the cover in water. Clean the vent by pulling a pipe cleaner through it. The pressure gauge should be checked for accuracy before the canning season begins. This ensures you of getting correct processing temperatures and a superior canned product.

Clean your water-bath canner thoroughly and dry it well before storing.

Store all your canning supplies together. On canning day everything will be right at hand.

Food — Make a list of the kinds and amounts of food you plan to can. The FOOD PLANNING GUIDE on page 178 will help you decide what kinds of food and what quantities of each to can. Plan on canning foods of superior quality. Fruits and vegetables should be ripe, fresh, and sound. Only freshly killed meat and poultry that have continually been chilled until ready to use should be canned. Seafood should be freshly caught.

Procedure —

1. Before starting to can, read the recipe and review the manufacturer's instructions for filling and sealing the jars. If applicable, reread the manufacturer's directions for the safe and successful operation of your steam-pressure canner.

2. Assemble all the necessary equipment and any clean cloths you'll need.

3. Wash jars and fittings (except self-sealing lids) in warm sudsy water; rinse well. Self-sealing lids should be washed according to manufacturer's directions. Or, place them in a pan and pour boiling water over them. Allow jars to sit in fresh hot water until ready to fill.

4. Prepare at one time only enough produce for a canner load. Consult your recipe for proper preparation of food. Pack jars according to type and the manufacturer's instructions. Add liquid according to recipe.

5. To remove air bubbles in filled jars, slide a table knife inside the jar and around the sides. This step helps prevent the liquid from falling below the level of the food during processing. Food tends to darken if not covered with liquid. After this step it may be necessary to add more liquid to cover the food.

6. Wipe mouths of jars with a clean, damp cloth to remove any food spilled on them.

7. Seal jars. Process them at once by the recommended method and for the correct length of time. See pages 6-8 and 180-182 for this information.

8. After processing, cool jars by setting them upright on a board, rack, or folded cloth — never on a cold surface. Place them far enough apart to allow air circulation. Don't expose them to a cold draft, and do not cover them.

9. After about 12 hours, test jars for sealing. If self-sealing lids are used, the center of the lid should be down (drawn in). Or, lid should remain down when pressed. Check jars with other kinds of closures by turning them partly over and examining for leakage. If a jar is imperfectly sealed, repack the food using a new lid and reprocess it for the full length of time. Or refrigerate the food and use it as soon as possible.

10. Wipe jars clean, label with food processed, and date. Store the jars in a cool, dry place away from danger of freezing, which may cause jar to crack or seal to break. Choose a dark area: exposed to light, food tends to lose natural color.

The chart below will help you in your planning and preparation. Columns 1 and 2 indicate the kind and amount of food to be canned; column 3 shows you approximately how many quart jars you'll need to can this quantity. Column 4 indicates the amount of food that a 1 quart jar holds.

JAR ESTIMATE GUIDE

RAW PRODUCE	MEASURE AND WEIGHT	APPROXIMATE NUMBER QUART JARS NEEDED	WEIGHT OR PRODUCE 1 QUART JAR HOLDS
FRUITS			
Apples	1 bu. (48 lbs.)	16-20	2½ to 3 lbs.
Apricots	1 lug or 1 box (22 lbs.)	7-11	2 to 2½ lbs.
Berries	24 quart crate	12-18	1½ to 3 lbs.
Cherries	1 bu. (56 lbs.)	22-32 (unpitted)	2 to 2½ lbs.
	1 lug (22 lbs.)	9-11 (unpitted)	2 to 2½ lbs.
Peaches	1 bu. (48 lbs.)	18-24	2 to 3 lbs.
	1 lug (22 lbs.)	8-12	2 to 3 lbs.
Pears	1 bu. (50 lbs.)	20-25	2 to 3 lbs.
	1 box (35 lbs.)	14-17	2 to 3 lbs.
Plums	1 bu. (56 lbs.)	24-30	1½ to 2½ lbs.
	1 lug (24 lbs.)	12	1½ to 2½ lbs.
Tomatoes	1 bu. (53 lbs.)	15-20	2½ to 3½ lbs.
	1 lug (30 lbs.)	10	2½ to 3½ lbs.
VEGETABLES			
Beans, Lima (in pods)	1 bu. (32 lbs.)	6-10	3 to 5 lbs.
Beans, Green or Wax	1 bu. (30 lbs.)	12-20	1½ to 2½ lbs.
Carrots (without tops)	1 bu. (50 lbs.)	16-25	2 to 3 lbs.
Corn, Sweet (in husks)	1 bu. (35 lbs.)	6-10 (whole-kernel)	3 to 6 lbs.
Peas, Green (in pods)	1 bu. (30 lbs.)	5-10	3 to 6 lbs.
Spinach and other greens	1 bu. (18 lbs.)	3-8	2 to 6 lbs.
Squash, Summer	1 bu. (40 lbs.)	10-20	2 to 4 lbs.
Sweet Potatoes	1 bu. (50 lbs.)	16-25	2 to 3 lbs.
MEATS			
Steer (prime quality)	3 lbs.	3	
Hog	3 lbs.	3	
Chicken (with bone)	3-4 lbs.	1	

Spiced Peaches (page 25)
Peach Conserve (page 117)

fruits and juices

Virtually every southern home either has some fruit trees or has ready access to a supply of garden-fresh fruits. Southern homemakers often can or preserve fruits as a summer activity. They can fruit and prepare juices from fruit as well. To preserve many of these foods, they'll depend on generations-old recipes. Recipes that have been in their families longer than anyone remembers.

To complement these recipes, they'll rely on up-to-the-minute instructions for preserving fruit. Instructions like those you'll find in the following pages. Accompanying these instructions are many of the treasured recipes referred to above. In fact, for canning and preserving fruits and juices, the recipes and instructions in this section form an unbeatable combination.

Try preparing Spiced Oranges for a delicious, tart blend of fruit and seasonings your family will enjoy at every meal, even breakfast. And for old-fashioned flavor, preserve Brandied Peaches and serve them up to accompany a holiday roast. You'll also want to prepare fruit butters, those rich combinations of fruit and sweetening so like creamery butter they're used to top toast or biscuits. And don't ignore the possibilities of preparing your very own juices. You'll find recipes for old-time Blackberry Cordial . . . Grape Juice . . . and Tomato Juice Cocktail. In fact, you'll find so many easy-to-prepare home-tested recipes, you won't know which one to try first!

Fruits are processed in a water-bath canner at the temperature of boiling water. Because fruits have a high acid content, processing at the boiling point of water is sufficient to ensure that all bacteria are destroyed. At higher temperatures the flavor and vitamin content of the fruit will be affected.

Sugar syrups are the preservatives frequently used in canning fruits. They are especially effective in preserving the shape, flavor, and color of the produce. The density of the syrup you use will vary according to the character of the fruit to be canned. Specific recipe directions will give you the appropriate information on the type of syrup to be used. For each pint of fruit, allow 2/3 cup syrup; for each quart of produce, 1 to 1 1/3 cups will suffice.

The following table details the accepted sugar (or corn syrup or honey) to water ratios for the various syrups.

instructions

FOR FRUITS

SYRUPS FOR CANNING		
Type of Syrup	Sugar to One Quart Water	Yield of Syrup
Light	2 cups	5 cups
Medium	3 cups	5 1/2 cups
Heavy	4 3/4 cups	6 1/2 cups
Medium with Corn Syrup: 1 1/2 cups sugar, 1 cup syrup to 3 cups water.		
Medium with Honey: 1 cup sugar, 1 cup honey to 4 cups water.		

GENERAL INSTRUCTIONS

1. Read your recipe carefully. Check the manufacturer's instructions for filling and sealing the canning jars.
2. Gather together all the utensils that you will need. Fill the water-bath canner half full with hot water and put it on the stove to heat.
3. Check the jars for nicks, cracks, and sharp edges on the sealing surfaces. Discard any damaged jars. Wash the jars in hot soapy water and rinse. Allow the jars to remain in a pan of hot water. They can be boiled until ready to use. Wash and rinse fittings.
4. Select sound, fresh, firm-ripe fruits. Sort them for size, ripeness, and color. Wash the produce thoroughly under cold running water or in several changes of water. Drain the fruit.
5. Remove the hulls, cores, pits, seeds, or skins. If the fruit you are canning has delicate, light-colored flesh that will darken upon exposure to the air (apples, apricots, peaches, and pears), you should drop them into one of these solutions before packing. There are four such solu-

tions that can be used: a sugar syrup; ascorbic acid or ascorbic acid mixture used according to the manufacturer's instructions; 1 teaspoon citric acid mixed in 1 gallon water; or a vinegar-salt solution prepared from 2 tablespoons each salt and vinegar to 1 gallon water. Don't allow the fruit to sit in any of these solutions for more than 15 minutes. Fruit that has been allowed to sit in a vinegar-salt mixture needs rinsing.

6. Prepare the sugar syrup. Measure sugar and liquid (either water or fruit juice) into saucepan. Cook until the sugar dissolves. Keep the syrup hot until it is needed, but do not let it boil down.

7. There are two ways to pack fruit for canning. If your recipe specifies a *raw pack*, place the raw fruit into clean canning jars and cover with hot syrup, fruit juice, or water. Pack all raw foods tightly because they shrink during processing. For a *hot pack*, before packing heat the fruit in syrup, water, or extracted juice. Have the produce at or near the boiling point when filling the jars. Pack rather loosely. Leave 1/2 inch head space in each of the jars.

8. Remove any air bubbles from the canning jar by running a table knife or metal spatula between the jar and the food. This step helps prevent the liquid from falling below the level of the fruit during processing. If the produce is not completely covered with liquid, the food darkens.

9. To prevent darkening of the fruit in the jar, use ascorbic or citric acid mixtures prepared according to the manufacturer's instructions. If you choose pure undiluted ascorbic acid, before capping the jar sprinkle 1/4 teaspoon over each quart of fruit.

10. Wipe the top and threads of the jar with a clean damp cloth before capping. Seal the jars according to the manufacturer's instructions.

11. While you have been working, the canner, which has been half-filled with water, has been heating on the stove. After you fill and seal each jar, place it on the canner rack in the hot but not boiling water. When all the jars are in the canner add water to cover 1 to 2 inches above the tops of the jars. Cover the canner.

12. Heat the water to a full boil. When the water is boiling, begin to count the processing time.

13. Reduce the heat but maintain a steady but gentle boil. Process the fruit for the recipe's recommended length of time. If tops of jars become exposed, add boiling water to cover them 1 to 2 inches.

14. Remove the jars from the canner after the proper amount of processing time has elapsed. Allow them to cool on a surface of cloth or wood, a few inches apart, away from drafts. About 12 hours later, test the seals of the jars. To test a seal look to see if the lid is sunk in the middle. If it is not, press down middle. If middle stays down jar is sealed. If for any reason a jar has failed to seal, repack and reprocess it for the full length of time. Or refrigerate the jar and use the contents as soon as possible.

15. Wipe the jars thoroughly. Label them with the type of produce and the date on which it was canned.

16. Store the jars in a cool, dry, dark place.

Fruits and Juices

Canned Nectarines (below), Strawberry Preserves (page 125)

CANNED NECTARINES

3 lb. firm ripe nectarines	1/4 tsp. salt
5 3/4 c. sugar	1 tart orange
1/4 c. light corn syrup	1/2 tsp. almond extract

Wash, drain, peel and cut the nectarines into halves. Weigh the fruit. Three pounds will be needed with remaining ingredients. Combine the nectarines, sugar, syrup and salt in a large kettle and cook over low heat until the sugar dissolves. Remove from heat and let stand for 2 or 3 hours. Bring to a boil and boil rapidly for 10 minutes. Slice the orange paper thin and add to the boiling mixture. Boil until the fruit is glossy and translucent when lifted from the syrup. Pour into a deep bowl and cover. Let stand for 24 to 48 hours, then return to the kettle. Discard the orange and add the almond extract. Boil for 5 minutes, then skim off foam quickly and pour the hot preserves to 1/4 inch of the top of the fruit jar. Wipe off anything spilled on the top or threads of the jar. Place a lid on the jar and screw the band tight. Let cool overnight, then lay jars on side for several days, turning each day, if the nectarines rise in the syrup.

CANNING APPLES

8 c. sliced apples	3/4 c. sugar

16

Wash, peel and core the apples. Slice thinly into a container with a cover and add a small amount of water. Cover and bring to a boil. Steam until the apples are soft, then mash. Add 1 cup sugar to each gallon apple pulp, then bring to a boil. Pack in hot sterilized jars to 1/2 inch from top. Place lids and rings on the jars. Process in a waterbath canner for 10 minutes. Remove jars from water and cool away from drafts.

Mrs. Betty Johnson, Mobile, Alabama

APPLE BUTTER WITH APPLE CIDER

5 lb. ripe tart apples	1 tsp. allspice
2 c. apple cider	1 tbsp. cinnamon
4 c. sugar	1/2 tsp. nutmeg
1 tsp. ground cloves	

Wash the apples thoroughly, then cut in quarters. Place the apples and 7 cups water in a large kettle and cook for 15 minutes or until soft. Press the apples through a sieve. Boil the cider until reduced by 1/2, then add to the apple puree. Combine the puree mixture, sugar, cloves, allspice, cinnamon and nutmeg and cook, stirring frequently, over low heat for about 1 hour or until thick. Pour into hot sterilized jars, leaving 1/4 inch head space and position the caps. Process for 10 minutes at 212 degrees in a waterbath canner. 4-5 pints.

Mrs. Mary Anne McConnell, Richmond, Virginia

APPLE PIE FILLING

2 c. sugar	3 qt. sliced apples
1 c. water	1 tsp. cinnamon
4 tbsp. cornstarch	

Combine the sugar, water and cornstarch in a saucepan, then cook and stir until smooth. Add the apples and cinnamon and cook until tender. Pack in sterilized jars and process at 5 pounds pressure in a pressure cooker for 10 minutes or in a water bath for 20 minutes.

Mrs. Hattie North, Jackson, Mississippi

APPLE RINGS

2 tsp. red food coloring	1 c. water
4 tbsp. lemon juice	4 whole cloves
2 c. sugar	1 lb. apples

Combine the food coloring, lemon juice, sugar, water and cloves in a saucepan and bring to a boil. Pare and core the apples, then cut into rings. Drop the rings immediately into the syrup to prevent discoloration. Cook, turning occasionally, over low heat until the apples are transparent. Pack in half-pint jars and pour in boiling syrup. Adjust jar lids and process at 212 degrees for 5 minutes in a waterbath canner.

Kay O'Neal Deckard, Swan Quarter, North Carolina

Apple Jelly from Bottled Juice (below); Easy Apple Butter (below); Apple Relish (page 146)

EASY APPLE BUTTER

4 c. canned applesauce	1 tsp. cinnamon
2 tbsp. lemon juice	1 c. (packed) brown sugar
1/2 tsp. grated orange rind	1/4 tsp. allspice
1/2 tsp. ground cloves	

Combine all the ingredients in a saucepan, then simmer, stirring occasionally, for 1 hour. Cool. Pour into sterilized glass jars.

APPLE JELLY FROM BOTTLED JUICE

2 pkg. or 2 tbsp. unflavored gelatin	2 tbsp. unsweetened lemon juice
1 qt. unsweetened apple juice	2 tbsp. liquid sweetener
	Food coloring, if desired

In a saucepan soften gelatin in apple juice and lemon juice. Bring to a rolling boil, dissolving gelatin. Boil for 1 minute. Remove from heat and stir in liquid sweetener and food coloring. Pour into hot sterilized jars. Seal. Store in refrigerator. About 2 pints.

APRICOTS

Sugar	Apricots

Prepare a thin syrup by combining 1 cup sugar per 2 cups water in a saucepan and bringing to a boil. Allow 1 to 1 1/3 cups syrup for each quart jar. Immerse the apricots in boiling water for 1 minute, then cool in cold water and slip skins off. Apricots may be canned whole or cut in halves as desired. Peeling may be omitted. Pack whole or halved apricots in sterilized jars and cover with boiling syrup, leaving 1/2 inch space at top of jar. Place lids on jars and tighten. Process in boiling water in a waterbath canner for 30 minutes. Process pint jars for 25 minutes.

Mrs. Anna Joyce, Houston, Texas

APRICOT BUTTER

5 lb. apricots	Juice and grated rind of 1 orange
6 c. sugar	Mixed spices

Peel and pit the apricots and cut in small pieces. Combine the apricots, sugar and orange juice and rind in a large kettle and cook over low heat until of a thick spreading consistency. Two teaspoons mixed whole spices per gallon of butter may be added after the apricots are soft. Tie the spices in a bag for easy removal. Pour into hot sterilized jars and adjust the lids. Process for 10 minutes in a boiling water bath.

Mrs. Sarah North, Flagstaff, Arizona

BLACKBERRIES

6 gal. blackberries	12 c. sugar

Wash the blackberries and drain well. Work with a small amount at a time to prevent the blackberries from soaking. Combine the berries and sugar in a large pan and cover, then bring to a boil. Pack in hot sterilized jars to within 1/2 inch of top, making certain juice covers the blackberries. Adjust the jar lids and process pints for 10 minutes and quarts for 15 minutes in boiling water in a waterbath canner. Canned blackberries may be served cold or combined with other berries and fruits for breakfast. Pie filling may be made by adding a thickening agent and desired spices.

Mrs. Carolyn Smith, Decatur, Alabama

CRANBERRIES

Sugar	Cranberries

Combine 1 1/4 cups sugar and 1 cup water to make a heavy syrup. Prepare enough syrup to allow 1 to 1 1/3 cups per quart jar. Wash and remove stems from the cranberries, then boil for 3 minutes in the heavy syrup. Pack in hot sterilized jars and cover with boiling syrup. Process for 3 minutes in a boiling water bath.

Mrs. Rita Anderson, Little Rock, Arkansas

Spiced Oranges (below)

SPICED ORANGES

4 Florida oranges	12 whole cloves
2 c. sugar	3 sticks cinnamon, broken
1/2 c. vinegar	

Add enough water to whole oranges to cover in saucepan, then bring to a boil. Boil for 20 minutes or until easily pierced with a fork. Drain and cut into eighths. Combine the sugar, 1 1/4 cups water, vinegar, cloves and cinnamon in a large saucepan, then simmer, stirring constantly, until the sugar is dissolved. Bring to a boil, then add the orange pieces and simmer about 20 minutes. Spoon into hot sterilized jars and seal.

Photographs for this recipe above and on page 114.

SPICED ORANGE WEDGES

12 oranges	3 2-in. sticks cinnamon
4 c. sugar	1 1/2 tsp. whole allspice

Cut each orange into 6 wedges and place in a large bowl. Add water to cover and let stand for 3 to 4 hours. Drain the oranges, reserving oranges and 1 quart liquid. Combine the liquid, sugar and spices in a large saucepan. Bring to boiling point and boil for 5 minutes. Add the oranges and bring to a boil, then reduce the heat. Simmer, uncovered, for 20 minutes or until the skins are slightly transparent. Pack the oranges and spices in hot sterilized jars. Fill to within 1/2 inch of top with syrup. Seal immediately. Serve as meat accompaniment. 8 half-pint jars.

Photograph for this recipe on page 5.

MARASCHINO CHERRIES

4 1/2 lb. Royal Anne cherries	1 oz. red food coloring
2 tbsp. salt	Juice of 1 lemon
1 tbsp. powdered alum	1 oz. almond extract
4 1/2 lb. sugar	

Soak pitted cherries overnight in water to cover with salt and alum. Wash well in cold water and drain. Add 2 cups cold water. Add the sugar and food coloring and bring to boiling point. Remove from heat and let stand for 24 hours. Repeat for 2 mornings, bringing all to a boil. Add the lemon juice and almond extract on the third morning and bring to a boil. Place in sterilized jars and adjust lids and rings. Process in boiling water in a waterbath canner for 5 minutes. 12 half-pints.

Mrs. Margaret Clay, Durham, North Carolina

CHERRY OLIVES

2 lb. fresh Bing cherries	3 c. water
1 c. vinegar	3 tbsp. salt
1 tbsp. sugar	

Wash and pack the cherries into sterilized jars. Combine remaining ingredients in a saucepan and cook just enough to dissolve the salt and sugar. Cool and pour over cherries. Place lids and rings on jars and process in boiling water for 10 minutes. 6 pints.

Mrs. Patsy Howsley Mayer, Kermit, Texas

RED CINNAMON CRAB APPLES

Crab apples with stems	1 1/2 c. red hot cinnamon
4 c. water	candies
1 c. sugar	

Pack the crab apples in sterilized jars. Combine the water, sugar and candies in a saucepan and boil until candies are melted, then pour over apples. Place the lids on the jars and screw tightly. Place on a rack in a container deep enough to allow water to come 2 inches above the jar tops. Process in boiling water for 20 minutes. Remove jars from water and cool away from drafts.

Mrs. Mary Cramton, Dothan, Alabama

GRAPES

Ripe grapes	Light or med. syrup

Wash and drain the grapes, then remove the stems. Pour about 1/2 cup boiling syrup into a hot sterilized jar, then fill the jar with grapes. Add more syrup, if necessary, to fill jar to 1/2 inch from top. Place tops on jars immediately after filling. Process pints for 15 minutes and quarts for 20 minutes in a boiling water bath.

Mabel Williams, Portales, New Mexico

SPICED GRAPE BUTTER

4 lb. ripe grapes	Gingerroot
10 whole cloves	1/2 c. vinegar
12 allspice	Sugar
1 stick of cinnamon	

Wash and stem the grapes, then mash. Tie the spices in a bag and add to the mashed grapes. Cook until the grapes are soft and discard the spice bag. Press the grapes through a sieve and measure the pulp. Add the vinegar and 1 cup sugar to each 2 cups pulp. Cook and stir until the butter is thick. Pour into hot jars and process for 10 minutes in a boiling water bath.

Mrs. Edwin Nelson, Natchez, Mississippi

CABANA BANANA BUTTER

4 lge. bananas	1/2 tsp. ground cinnamon
2 tbsp. lemon juice	1/8 tsp. ground cloves
1 1/2 c. sugar	

Peel the bananas and cut into chunks, then sprinkle with the lemon juice. Mash in blender or electric mixer. Combine with the sugar and spices in a large saucepan. Bring to a boil, then simmer, stirring constantly for 15 minutes. Spoon into sterilized jars and seal. Store in cool place. Will keep for several weeks.

Cabana Banana Butter (above)

GRAPEFRUIT

Sugar   Firm tree-ripened grapefruit

Combine 2 cups sugar and 4 cups water in a saucepan and boil, stirring, until the sugar is dissolved. Pare the grapefruit, cutting deep enough to remove the white membrane. Remove the pulp from each section and discard the seed. Pack the grapefruit into hot sterilized jars and cover with boiling syrup to 1/2 inch from top of jars. Place the caps and rings on the jars and tighten. Process for 10 minutes in a boiling water bath.

Mrs. Marie Fernandez, Galveston, Texas

GRAPE BUTTER

Grapes   Sugar

Wash the grapes carefully and remove the stems. Add enough water to prevent grapes from sticking and simmer until tender. Press the pulp through a strainer to remove the seeds. Measure the puree and add 1/2 cup sugar per cup puree. Cook, stirring frequently, until of thick spreading consistency. Pour in hot sterilized jars and remove any air bubbles by sliding a table knife all the way around the inside of the jars. Place the lids on the jars and tighten. Process in a boiling water bath for 10 minutes.

Mrs. Virginia Hackworth, Atlanta, Georgia

FIGS

Tree-ripened figs with stems   Medium or heavy syrup

Wash the figs, then cover with boiling water and let stand for 3 to 4 minutes. Drain. Pack the hot figs to within 1/2 inch of the top of the jars and cover with boiling syrup. Adjust jar lids and process for 35 minutes in pint jars or 1 hour in quart jars at 10 pounds pressure.

Mrs. Louise Castleberry, San Antonio, Texas

BUFFET FIGS

6 qt. figs   6 c. honey
1 c. soda

Select firm ripe figs. Combine the soda and 1 gallon boiling water and pour over the figs. Soak for about 10 minutes or until skins become transparent, then rinse in cold water. Combine the honey and 6 cups water for syrup and bring to a boil. Add the figs to the syrup and simmer until figs are clear. Pack in hot sterilized jars and cover with boiling syrup. Add lemon slices to each jar, if desired. Place lids and rings on jars and process for 25 minutes in a boiling water bath.

Mrs. Sara Kinney, Montgomery, Alabama

Old-Fashioned Figs (below)

OLD-FASHIONED FIGS

2 lb. dried figs	2 sticks cinnamon
2 c. (packed) brown sugar	3 whole cloves
1/2 c. lemon juice	1 lemon, thinly sliced

Place the figs in a large saucepan, then stir in the remaining ingredients. Bring to a boil and cook for 15 minutes. Fill hot sterilized jars with figs, then cover with the syrup. Seal.

GUAVA BUTTER

5 lb. guavas	1 tsp. allspice
2 c. apple cider	1 tbsp. cinnamon
4 c. sugar	1/2 tsp. nutmeg
1 tsp. cloves	

Wash the guavas carefully and cut in quarters. Cover with 7 cups water and cook until the guavas are soft. Press the guavas through a fine sieve. The puree should measure about 2 quarts. Boil the apple cider until it is reduced by 1 cup and add to the guava puree. Add the sugar and spices and bring to a boil. Cook and stir over low heat until the guava mixture is of a thin spreading consistency. Pour into hot sterilized jars up to 1/4 inch from tops. Place the lids and rings on the jars and tighten. Process for 10 minutes in boiling water in a waterbath canner. About 5 pints.

Mrs. John A. Hines, Mobile, Alabama

BRANDIED PEACHES

2 c. sugar	6 to 8 sm. fresh peaches,
2 c. water	peeled
1 2-in. stick cinnamon	Brandy

Combine the sugar, water and cinnamon in a medium saucepan and bring to boiling point. Boil over high heat for 5 minutes. Add several peaches at a time and cook for 5 to 10 minutes or until peaches can be easily pierced with a fork. Remove the peaches from the syrup and pack in hot sterilized jars. Continue with remaining peaches till all have been cooked. Boil the syrup until 222 degrees is reached on a candy thermometer, then cool and add 1 pint brandy for each pint of syrup. Fill the jars with the brandy syrup and seal immediately.

Mrs. Martha Lewis, Columbia, South Carolina

PEACHES

Sugar	2 tbsp. vinegar
2 tbsp. salt	Peaches

Combine 3 cups sugar and 5 1/2 cups water in a saucepan and boil, stirring, until the sugar is dissolved. Combine salt, vinegar and 1 quart water in a large container. Place peaches in a wire basket or cheesecloth and plunge into boiling water just long enough to loosen skins. Cut in halves and remove the pit, then peel. Drop into vinegar mixture to prevent darkening until all the peaches are ready for canning. Do not leave peaches in vinegar mixture longer than 20 minutes. Drain. Cook several peaches at a time in the boiling syrup until heated through, then pack in hot jars, leaving 1/2 inch head space. Cover the peaches with boiling syrup and adjust the caps and rings. Process pints for 20 minutes and quarts for 25 minutes at 212 degrees in a waterbath canner.

Mrs. M. L. Bruce, Macon, Georgia

SPICED PEACHES

Firm ripe peaches	1/2 tsp. whole allspice
3 c. sugar	1/3 whole nutmeg
1/2 tsp. whole cloves	2 sticks cinnamon

Wash and rinse the peaches and set aside to drain. Combine the sugar and 4 cups water in a large saucepan. Tie the spices in a piece of cloth and add to the sugar and water. Bring to a boil and boil, stirring, until the sugar dissolves. Leave spice bag in syrup while preparing the peaches. Dip the peaches in boiling water until the skins slip easily, then plunge into cold water. Peel, but do not pit. Pack the peaches to within 1/2 inch of the top of the jar. Tapered jars are ideal for easy removal of whole peaches. Remove the spice bag from the syrup and bring the syrup to a boil. Cover the peaches with the boiling syrup and place the lid on the jar, then screw the band tight. Process pints for 25 minutes and quarts for 30 minutes in boiling water in a waterbath canner.

Photograph for this recipe on page 12.

PEACH BUTTER

Ripe peaches   Ginger
Sugar   Nutmeg

Scald, pit, peel and chop the peaches. Cook, in just enough water to prevent sticking, until soft and press through a sieve. Measure the pulp and add 1/2 cup sugar to each cup of pulp. Cook and stir for about 30 minutes or until thick and clear. One-half to 1 teaspoon each of ginger and nutmeg may be added, if desired. Pour immediately into hot sterilized jars and cover with caps. Process in boiling water in a waterbath canner for 10 minutes.

Mrs. Mary E. Cain, Dallas, Texas

SALAD PEACHES

6 c. sugar   1 tsp. salt
4 c. vinegar   1/2 tsp. ground ginger
3 sticks cinnamon   1/2 tsp. mace
1 tbsp. whole cloves   8 lb. small firm peaches
1 tbsp. whole allspice

Combine all the ingredients except the peaches in a kettle, then bring to a boil. Simmer for about 30 minutes. Wash and scald the peaches for 1 minute in boiling water, then dip in cold water, drain and peel. Add the peaches, several at a time, to the syrup, then boil gently for 4 or 5 minutes. Pack hot peaches to within 1/2 inch of top of sterilized fruit jar, then cover with hot syrup. Seal the jar and process for 20 minutes in boiling water.

Salad Peaches (above), Peach Jam (page 91)

STUFFED LEMONS

Lemons	4 tbsp. red food coloring
2 pt. vinegar	2 tbsp. cassia buds
3 pt. sugar	2 c. dried figs
1 c. lemon juice	2 c. raisins
1 pt. grenadine	2 c. nuts
2 4-in. pieces of cinnamon	1/2 c. maraschino cherries

Cut ends out of the lemons with a sharp knife. Remove all pulp through the holes and discard. Cover lemons with water and boil for 30 minutes, then drain. Cover again with water and boil for 20 minutes. Drain and repeat the process. Combine the vinegar, sugar, 1 cup water, lemon juice, grenadine, cinnamon, food coloring and cassia buds in a saucepan and add lemons. Simmer for 30 minutes or till the lemons are tender when pierced. Grind the figs, raisins, nuts and cherries for stuffing. Stuff lemons and plug the ends with 1/2 maraschino cherry. Pack in sterilized jars, then cover with pickling syrup. Seal. Process in a boiling water bath for 15 minutes. Slice with a sharp knife. Serve with meat or fowl.

Mrs. Gertrude Clay, Van Buren, Arkansas

KIEFFER PEARS

Yellow Kieffer pears	Sugar
Citric acid	

Store the pears in a single layer in a dry place at about 65 degrees for about 2 weeks. Storage improves the flavor and texture of hard pears. Wash, peel, halve and core the pears and drop into a solution of 1 teaspoon citric acid to 1 gallon water. Citric acid solution prevents the pears from darkening until the entire amount is ready for canning. Boil the pears in water to cover until tender. Use the water in which the pears are boiled and add 2 cups sugar to 4 cups water to make a thin syrup. Boil the pears in the syrup for 4 to 8 minutes. Pack to 1/2 inch from top of jars, then cover with boiling syrup, leaving 1/2 inch for expansion during processing. Place the lids on the jars and tighten. Process in a boiling water bath for 20 minutes in pint jars and 25 minutes in quart jars.

Mrs. Frank Meadows, Searcy, Arkansas

CINNAMON PEARS

2 qt. water	1/2 lge. bottle red food
1 pkg. red hot candies	coloring
4 cinnamon sticks	4 qt. (about) peeled pears,
6 whole cloves	halved or quartered
1 1/2 c. sugar	

Combine the first 6 ingredients in a large container and bring to a boil. Fill the pan with the pears and cook until tender. Remove the cinnamon and cloves. Fill pint or quart jars and seal while hot. Process for 15 minutes in a boiling water bath. About 4 quarts.

Mrs. O. L. Moos, Elkins, Arkansas

Cinnamon-Spiced Pears (below)

CINNAMON-SPICED PEARS

2 1-lb. 14-oz. cans pear
   halves
2 whole gingerroots, cracked
1/4 c. fresh lime juice

1/2 c. sugar
1/8 tsp. salt
3 2-in. sticks cinnamon

Drain the syrup from the pears into a saucepan. Soak the gingerroots in lime juice for 10 minutes. Add to the pear syrup with the sugar, salt and cinnamon. Bring to a boil and simmer for 15 minutes. Add the pear halves and cook, uncovered, for 15 minutes. Pack in hot sterilized jars, filling to within 1/2-inch from top. Seal at once. Serve with meat or poultry.

PEAR HONEY BUTTER

4 c. pear puree
1 c. sugar

1 1/4 c. strained honey
1 tbsp. lemon juice

Combine all the ingredients in a heavy bottomed container. Cook and stir for about 15 minutes or until thickened. Pour immediately into hot jars, leaving room for expansion and place the caps, then tighten. Process in boiling water for 10 minutes. The butter will thicken after cooling.

Mrs. Alice Palmer, Cleveland, Mississippi

PEAR BUTTER

18 to 20 ripe pears
3 c. sugar
1/3 c. orange juice

1 tsp. grated orange rind
1/2 tsp. nutmeg

Wash the pears carefully. Quarter or slice and remove the cores. Add just enough water to prevent the pears from sticking and cook until soft. Press through a fine sieve or food mill. Measure the pulp. Add remaining ingredients and cook for about 15 minutes or until thick. Pour into hot sterilized jars, leaving 1/4 inch head space. Process for 10 minutes at 212 degrees in a waterbath canner. About 2 pints.

Mrs. Clara Hamilton, Fort Payne, Alabama

PERSIMMONS

Ripe persimmons   **Sugar to taste**

Wash the persimmons, then place in a saucepan with a small amount of water and cover. Boil until persimmons are soft, then press through a sieve. Sweeten the pulp and bring to a boil. Pour boiling pulp into hot jars and stir with a rubber scraper to remove air bubbles. Place a cap and ring on each jar after filling and place in a waterbath canner. Process pints for 15 minutes and quarts for 20 minutes in boiling water.

Mrs. Barbara Jones, Montgomery, Alabama

PINEAPPLE

Sugar   **Firm ripe pineapple**

Prepare a light syrup with 2 cups sugar and 1 quart water. Boil and stir until the sugar is dissolved. Cut a thin slice from the bottom of the pineapple, then cut into 1/2-inch slices, crosswise. Peel, then remove the core with a doughnut cutter, if available. Drop the slices into the syrup and simmer until tender. Pack the hot pineapple slices in hot jars, leaving 1/2-inch head space and cover with boiling syrup. Adjust jar caps and process pints for 15 minutes and quarts for 20 minutes in boiling water in a waterbath canner.

Mrs. John Pothoff, Stuart, Florida

PLUMS

Plums   **Medium syrup**

Select and wash just ripe plums, then prick the skins with a needle to help prevent the plums from bursting. Plums may be peeled, but a more attractive product is obtained without peeling. Bring the syrup to a boil and add plums. Cook for 2 minutes, then remove from heat and cover. Let plums stand in syrup for 20 to 30 minutes, then pack in hot jars, leaving 1/2 inch at top of jars. Pour boiling syrup over plums to 1/2 inch from top of jars and adjust caps. Process pints for 20 minutes and quarts for 25 minutes in boiling water in a waterbath canner.

Mrs. Ed Brown, Jackson, Mississippi

APRICOT PUREE

Ripe apricots   **Lemon juice**
Sugar

Wash, drain, pit and measure the apricots. Place in a large kettle and add 1 cup boiling water for each quart apricots. Cook until apricots are soft, then strain through a sieve. Add about 1 1/3 cups sugar and 1 tablespoon lemon juice per quart puree. Cook and stir until the sugar dissolves, then pour hot puree into hot jars up to 1/4 inch from top of jars. Place jar caps and rings according to package directions. Process for 15 minutes in boiling water in a waterbath canner. Puree may be thinned with ice water to serve as a beverage.

Mrs. Wayne C. Hill, Clovis, New Mexico

BLACKBERRY CORDIAL

4 qt. blackberries   **1 tbsp. whole cinnamon**
3 c. sugar   **1 tbsp. whole nutmeg**
1 tbsp. whole cloves

Crush the blackberries and simmer until soft. Strain through a cloth or jelly bag and measure. About 2 quarts juice should be the yield. Add the sugar to the juice, stirring until sugar is dissolved. Tie the spices in a bag and drop into the juice. Simmer for 30 minutes, then discard the spice bag. Bring juice to a boil and pour immediately into hot sterilized jars, leaving 1/4 inch head space. Adjust caps and tighten.

Mrs. Lane Meadows, Meridian, Mississippi

CRANBERRY JUICE

Cranberries   **Sugar**

Wash and remove stems from the cranberries, then cover with water. Boil for about 5 minutes or until the skins burst. Strain through cheesecloth, but do not squeeze. Measure the juice and add 2/3 cup sugar for each quart. Bring to boiling point and pour immediately into hot sterilized jars. Process at 180 degrees in a waterbath for 20 minutes.

Mrs. Lisa Scott, Covington, Kentucky

WILD CHERRY DRINK

Ripe chokecherries   **Sugar**

Crush the cherries and cover with water. Let stand for 10 hours or overnight. Drain the cherry juice through a bag or cloth, then add 1/2 cup sugar to each quart juice. Bring to a boil. Pour into sterilized jars and seal. Process in a boiling water bath for 5 minutes.

Mrs. Claire Martin, Durham, North Carolina

GRAPE JUICE

Grapes   **Sugar**

Wash and remove any green or spoiled grapes. Weigh the sound grapes and place in a boiler. Add 1 cup water to each 5 pounds grapes. Simmer for 5 minutes, then strain through fine cloth or a jelly bag, pressing out all juice. Measure the juice and add 1/2 cup sugar for each quart juice. Bring to simmering temperature, stirring until the sugar is dissolved. Pour into sterilized containers and adjust jar lids. Process in 190-degree water in a waterbath canner for 30 minutes.

Mrs. R. B. Freeman, Nashville, North Carolina

GRAPEFRUIT JUICE

Tree-ripened grapefruit   **Sugar to taste**

Wash the grapefruit thoroughly, then extract and strain the juice. Add sugar and cook, stirring until sugar is dissolved, to 165 degrees. Pour the hot juice into hot jars, leaving 1/4 inch head space, then place caps on the jars. Process at 165 degrees in a waterbath canner for 30 minutes. Store in a cool, dark place, if possible.

Mrs. Jane Carey, St. Augustine, Florida

TOMATO JUICE COCKTAIL

1 bushel ripe tomatoes,   **6 med. onions, chopped**
  quartered   **1 c. sugar**
3 bunches celery, chopped   **3/4 c. salt**
6 med. green peppers, chopped

Place the tomatoes, celery, green peppers and onions in a large kettle. Cook until vegetables are tender, then strain. Mix the strained juice, sugar and salt and bring to a boil. Pour into sterilized jars and adjust jar lids. Process for 10 minutes at 212 degrees in a waterbath canner. 16 quarts.

Mrs. Glenn McCoy, Bonham, Texas

VEGETABLE COCKTAIL

2 qt. tomatoes, finely cut   **1 tbsp. salt**
1/4 green pepper, chopped   **1 tbsp. sugar**
2 med. onions, finely   **1/2 tsp. black pepper**
  chopped   **2 tbsp. lemon juice**
1 bay leaf   **2 tbsp. vinegar**
7 whole cloves

Combine the tomatoes, green pepper, onions, 1 cup water, bay leaf and cloves and simmer for 1 hour. Strain. Stir in remaining ingredients and bring to a boil. Pour into jars and seal while hot. Chill before serving.

Mrs. Thurman Lutrell, Altheimer, Arkansas

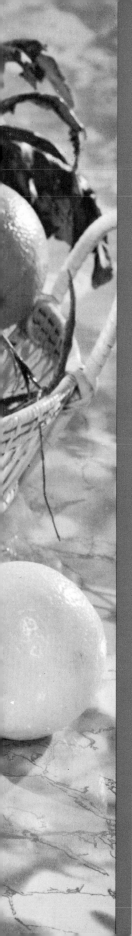

Beets (page 43)
Beet Relish (page 148)

vegetables

Homemakers throughout the Southland take enormous pride in the vegetables they grow and preserve. They enjoy opening a jar of corn they canned in the heat of July and bringing all that fresh flavor to a wintertime table. These women know that nothing beats the flavor of fresh canned vegetables — and also that canning is an excellent way to preserve all the food values in vegetables.

The collection of home-tested and proven canning recipes in the pages that follow is prefaced by pages of illustrated instructions on just how to can vegetables. These careful, step-by-step instructions are designed to help you can your garden's produce easily and safely.

Use these instructions to prepare Sauerkraut Made in Jars, an old-time favorite that's especially appreciated by today's flavor-seeking families. When you want to prepare your own Tomato Paste . . . Baked Beans . . . Hominy . . . or just about any vegetable you can name, you'll find a recipe for it in this section. There are recipes, too, for mixtures of vegetables: Tomatoes and Okra . . . Mixed Vegetable Salad . . . and Succotash. And you'll discover some recipes for preserving foods that aren't exactly vegetables but can often be served like them — Rhubarb, Mushrooms, Pumpkins.

For marvelously flavored recipes to help you preserve your family's favorite vegetables at the peak of their flavor, depend on this section — every time!

Depending on their acid content, vegetables are home-canned by either the water-bath or the steam-pressure method. Vegetables that are high in acidity – for example, rhubarb, sauerkraut, and tomatoes – are processed in a water-bath canner. The water-bath procedure provides enough heat to destroy microorganisms that spoil high-acid food, but not too high a heat to affect the flavor and nutritive value of the vegetables. The water-bath method, however, is not recommended for processing low-acid vegetables such as beans, beets, carrots, corn, peas, and so on. This method does not provide a high enough temperature to destroy all the spoilage-causing bacteria of low-acid foods. Use the steam-pressure method to process low-acid

canning instructions

FOR VEGETABLES

vegetables; in it, foods are processed at a much higher temperature.

The general instructions outlined below will help you accomplish both procedures quickly, effortlessly, and successfully. The first eleven steps apply to both the water-bath and steam-pressure method. Successive steps for each method are then outlined separately. Also, always follow your individual recipe carefully. In particular, it will provide more specific directions for the preparation of the vegetables.

GENERAL INSTRUCTIONS

The water-bath and the steam-pressure method

1. Read your recipe carefully. Review the manufacturer's instructions for filling and sealing the canning jars.

2. Assemble all the equipment and utensils you'll need.

3. Wash jars in hot soapy water and rinse well. Put jars in hot water and let boil until ready to use. Wash and rinse fittings.

4. Select vegetables. Vegetables should be canned when they are garden-fresh, young, and tender for the most delicious flavor and the most desirable appearance.

5. Prepare the vegetables by washing thoroughly, rinsing, and draining before cutting or breaking the skin. Any dirt allowed to remain on the vegetables will carry bacteria that is particularly difficult to destroy during processing. To wash, place small amounts of vegetables in several changes of cold water, rinsing out washing pans between each change of

water. Lift the vegetables *out* of the water so that dirt is washed off them and will not be drained back over them. Don't allow vegetables to soak in the water; they may lose flavor and nutritive value or become soggy. Scrub root vegetables with a brush. For even cooking sort vegetables for size and ripeness. Always handle them gently to avoid bruising.

6. If the recipe you follow specifies precooking of the vegetables before packing, complete this step accordingly.

7. Pack jars with raw food or precooked hot food, depending on your recipe. Raw produce should be packed more tightly into the jars than hot food, since raw vegetables tend to shrink during processing. Pack hot foods rather loosely. They should be at or near the boiling point when packed.

8. At this time salt may or may not be added to the jars. When salt is added, usually 1 teaspoon per quart is used. This amount is too small to help prevent spoilage, but it does add flavor.

9. Cover the vegetables with fresh boiling water or if applicable with the water in which they were precooked. The cooking liquid restores nutrients that may have been lost when the vegetables were heated. If the cooking liquid is dark or strong-flavored, you'll probably prefer to use fresh boiling water. Leave 1-inch head space between the packed food and the closure. Too much solid food packed into the jar retards the passage of heat to the center of the jar. If heat does not reach the center of the jar during processing, organisms may not be killed and the produce will spoil.

10. Remove air bubbles from the filled jars by running a table knife around the sides of the jar. After this step, the water level may fall. If so, add more liquid to cover the food, making sure to leave appropriate head space.

11. Wipe tops and necks of jars with clean cloth before capping to remove any food that may have been spilled on them. Seal the jars according to manufacturer's instructions. The food is now ready to be processed by either the water-bath method or the steam-pressure method. The following 10 steps apply to the water-bath method; the next 10 steps to the steam-pressure method.

The water-bath method

1. Fill the water-bath canner half full with water and put it on the stove to heat. You may want to perform this step before you begin to prepare the acid vegetables. For vegetables to be packed cold and raw, the water must be hot, but not boiling; for hot-packed vegetables, have the water boiling.

2. Place filled jars on the rack in the canner. Space jars to permit water to circulate freely around each one.

3. Add enough boiling water to cover tops of jars 1 to 2 inches. Put cover back on canner.

4. Heat the water in the canner to a full rolling boil. At this moment start to count processing time.

5. Regulate the heat in order to maintain a gentle, steady boil during processing. Process the vegetables for the recommended length of time (see pages 180-182). If some water boils away and exposes the tops of the jars, add boiling water to cover tops of jars 1 to 2 inches. *Jars must be covered with water throughout processing.*

6. When processing time is up, remove the canner from the heat source. Then immediately remove jars from the canner.

7. Allow jars to cool naturally by placing them upright on a surface of cloth or wood. Position jars a few inches apart and out of cool drafts.

8. After about 12 hours, test the seals of jars. To test a seal look to see if the lid is sunk in the middle. If it is not press down middle. If middle stays down jar is sealed. If a jar has failed to seal, remove the food, repack it using a new lid, and reprocess it for the full length of time. Or, refrigerate the food and use it as soon as possible.

9. Wipe the jars until clean. Label and date.

10. Store the jars in a cool, dry, dark place.

The steam-pressure method

1. Fill the canner with 2 to 3 inches of water and heat. As each jar is filled, place it on the rack in the canner. Position jars so that steam can flow freely around each one. If you have 2 layers of jars in the canner, use a rack between each layer and stagger the upper one.

2. Fasten on canner cover securely.

3. Leave vent open for 10 minutes to allow steam inside canner to escape. Then close vent and bring pressure to 10 pounds (240 degrees). Start counting processing time at the moment this pressure is reached.

4. Process for recommended length of time (see pages 180-182), keeping pressure constant throughout processing by regulating the heat source. Don't open the vent or allow a cold draft to blow around the canner.

5. When processing is completed, remove the canner from your heat source. Let pressure fall naturally to 0.

6. Wait 2 minutes, then slowly open vent. Unfasten cover, tilting the far side up so that the steam escapes *away* from you.

7. Remove jars from canner one at a time. Stand them upright to cool.

8. Allow jars to cool for about 12 hours and then test the seals. To test a seal look to see if the lid is sunk in the middle. If it is not press down

middle. If middle stays down jar is sealed. If a jar has failed to seal, remove the food, repack it using a new lid, and reprocess it for the full length of time. Or, refrigerate the food and use it as soon as possible.

9. Wipe jars clean, label, and date.

10. Store jars in a dark, dry, cool place.

SPOILAGE OF CANNED VEGETABLES

Like all other home-canned foods, vegetables need careful examination for spoilage after you open the jars. If the food gives off an unnatural odor or if appearance is not characteristic, discard it immediately. Cloudy canning liquid and bulging jar caps are also signs of spoilage and the canned food should not be used. Even if none of these signs of spoilage are obvious to you, always boil the vegetables, covered, in the water they were canned in about 10 to 15 minutes before tasting.

PIMENTOS

Firm, ripe pimentos

Cover pimentos with water and boil for 3 to 5 minutes or until skin slips easily. Remove the skins, stem and blossom ends and seed with a thin knife. Flatten the pimentos and pack in horizontal layers in hot sterilized jars, leaving 1/2-inch head space. Add no liquid. Process 1/2 pints for 35 minutes and pints for 55 minutes in boiling water in a waterbath canner.

Mrs. Henry Gardner, Lexington, Kentucky

SAUERKRAUT MADE IN JARS

5 lb. cabbage   **3 1/2 tbsp. salt**

Shred cabbage fine and place with salt in a large pan, mixing well. Pack solidly in sterilized jars. Fill the jars with cold water to within 1/2 inch of jar tops and seal tightly. Sauerkraut will ferment for 3 to 4 days and be ready to use in 4 to 6 weeks.

Mrs. Vivian Stewart, West Memphis, Arkansas

SAUERKRAUT

Sound, mature cabbage heads   **Salt**

Remove outside leaves and core of cabbage heads and discard. Shred the cabbage fine and weigh. Add 3 tablespoons pure salt to every 5 pounds cabbage and press firmly into a large jar or tight keg. Cover with a white cloth and a plate. Fill a jar with water to use for a weight to keep the cabbage under the brine which forms as the salt draws juice from the cabbage. Place the prepared cabbage in a temperature of about 85 degrees. Move to a cooler place of about 68 to 72 degrees when fermentation starts. Remove scum every day. Sauerkraut will be yellowed and free of white spots when fermentation is completed. Heat cabbage to just under boiling point. Pack into hot jars and cover with brine. Adjust lids on jars and process for 20 minutes in a boiling water bath.

Mrs. Susan Ingalls, Fort Pierce, Florida

TOMATOES FOR SALAD

Tomatoes   **Fresh or canned tomato juice**

Select only firm, ripe tomatoes, free of spots, decay, cracks or growths. Wash the tomatoes before scalding. Place the tomatoes in a wire basket or cheesecloth and plunge in boiling water just long enough to loosen skins. Dip in cold water and drain. Cut out the cores and remove skins. Pack whole tomatoes in hot jars, leaving 1/2-inch head space. Pour hot tomato juice over tomatoes up to 1/2 inch from tops of jars. Adjust jar lids and process pints for 35 minutes and quarts for 45 minutes in boiling water in a waterbath canner.

Tomatoes for Salad (page 38), Vegetable Soup Mix (page 69)

STEWED TOMATOES

Firm ripe tomatoes	**1 c. sliced celery**
1 med. green pepper	**1 tbsp. sugar**
1/2 c. chopped onion	**2 tsp. salt**

Scald, core, skin and chop enough tomatoes to measure 4 quarts. Remove the stem and blossom ends from the green pepper and discard the seeds, then cut into small pieces. Combine all the ingredients in kettle and bring a boil. Pour in hot sterilized jars, leaving 1/2-inch head space, then seal. Process pint jars for 15 minutes and quarts for 20 minutes at 10 pounds pressure or 50 minutes in boiling water in a waterbath canner.

Photograph for this recipe on page 45.

EASY STEWED TOMATOES

1 qt. tomatoes, cut	**3 tbsp. chopped celery**
in chunks	**1 tsp. celery salt**
2 tbsp. chopped green pepper	**1 tsp. sugar**
2 tbsp. chopped onions	**1/4 tsp. salt**

Combine all ingredients in a large kettle and cook for 10 minutes, then pour into hot sterilized jars. Screw the caps on tight. Process pints for 15 minutes and quarts for 20 minutes at 10 pounds pressure in a pressure cooker.

Mrs. Dennis Farnham, Alexandria, Louisiana

TOMATO PASTE

6 qt. peeled, cored,	**2 bay leaves**
chopped tomatoes	**1 tbsp. salt**
1 c. chopped sweet red	**1 clove of garlic**
peppers	

Combine the tomatoes, peppers, bay leaves and salt in a large pan and cook over low heat for about 1 hour. Press through a sieve. Return to the large pan and add the garlic. Cook over low heat for about 2 hours or until desired thickness, then remove the garlic. Pour hot tomato paste into hot jars, leaving 1/4 inch head space and adjust lids. Process for 45 minutes at 212 degrees in a waterbath canner. About 8 half-pints.

Photograph for this recipe on page 45.

MARINATED ARTICHOKE HEARTS

2 c. artichoke hearts	**1 c. salad oil**
1/2 tsp. salt	**1/2 c. lemon juice**
2 slivers of lemon peel	**1/2 c. lime juice**
2 slivers of lime peel	**3 cloves of garlic, crushed**

Place the artichoke hearts and salt in a saucepan containing about 2 inches of water and bring to a boil. Cook until slightly tender. Pack in pint jars. Place a sliver of lemon and lime in each jar. Combine the oil, juices and garlic in a saucepan and bring to a boil. Pour immediately over the artichoke hearts and seal. Place caps on jars. Process for 20 minutes in a waterbath canner.

Mrs. Anna Maria Hart, Tempe, Arizona

ASPARAGUS

1 bushel asparagus   **Salt**

Wash the asparagus, then trim off the tough ends and thick scales and cut in 1-inch pieces. Place in a large pan and cover with boiling water. Boil for 2 to 3 minutes, uncovered. Pack the asparagus in hot jars, leaving 3/4-inch head space. Add 1 teaspoon salt to each jar and cover with boiling water in which asparagus was blanched. Place a lid on each jar immediately after filling. Process for 55 minutes at 10 pounds pressure in a pressure canner. 11 quarts.

Mrs. Farley Hunt, Hot Springs, Arkansas

ASPARAGUS STALKS

Asparagus   **Salt**

Select fresh, tender asparagus stalks and sort according to size. Wash thoroughly. Remove tough ends and scales and wash again. Tie in uniform bundles and stand upright in boiling water. Cover and boil for 3 minutes. Pack immediately into hot jars and add 1/2 teaspoon salt to each pint. Cover with boiling blanching water, leaving 1/2 inch head space and adjust lids. Process for 25 minutes at 10 pounds pressure.

Mrs. Ida Locke, Saint Petersburg, Florida

BAKED BEANS

1 qt. dried beans	**3 tbsp. sugar**
1/2 lb. salt pork	**2 tsp. salt**
1 qt. tomato juice	**1/4 tsp. mixed spices**

Sort and wash the dried beans, then cover with boiling water. Boil for 2 minutes. Remove from heat and let soak for 1 hour. Return to heat and bring to a boil. Drain and reserve the liquid. Cut the pork in 2-inch pieces. Fill the jars 3/4 full with the hot beans and add a piece of salt pork to each jar. Mix the remaining ingredients in a saucepan and bring to a boil. Pour sauce into each jar with beans to 1/2 inch from the top. Finish filling with reserved liquid, if needed. Place lids on jars and tighten the bands. Process pint jars for 1 hour and 5 minutes at 10 pounds pressure.

Honey Gwinner, Baltimore, Maryland

FRESH-FROM-THE-GARDEN BEANS

Fresh tender green beans   **Salt**

Wash the beans. Break off ends and remove strings. Break or cut into 1-inch pieces and pack tightly into sterilized jars to 1/2 inch from top. Add 1/2 teaspoon salt to pints and 1 teaspoon to quarts. Cover with boiling water, leaving 1/2 inch for head space. Place the lids on jars and tighten. Process pint jars for 20 minutes and quart jars for 25 minutes at 10 pounds pressure in a pressure canner.

Mrs. P. F. White, Gadsden, Alabama

LIMA BEANS

1 bushel lima beans   **Salt**

Wash, drain and shell tender young beans. Wash again after shelling. Cover with boiling water. Boil for 3 minutes and pack into hot jars, leaving 1 inch head space. Add 1/2 teaspoon salt to pints and 1 teaspoon to quarts. Cover with boiling water, leaving 1 inch head space. Place caps on jars immediately after filling. Process for 25 minutes at 10 pounds pressure. 6-8 quarts.

Mrs. Irma Reynolds, Montgomery, Alabama

CANNED BEANS

8 pt. beans   **Salt**

Cut enough clean beans to fill 8 pint jars and place in a large pan. Add enough water to cover the beans. Bring to a boil and boil for 5 minutes, then pack in

Canned Beans (above)

42

hot sterilized jars up to 1/2 inch from tops. Add 1/2 teaspoon salt to each jar, then cover with boiling liquid to within 1/2 inch from top of jars. Adjust caps and process for 20 minutes at 10 pounds pressure.

Photographs for this recipe on pages 42 and 45.

BEET SALAD

1 c. vinegar	2 c. brown sugar
1/2 c. (heaping) flour	24 beets, cooked and
2 tbsp. mustard	cubed
1 tsp. salt	1 tsp. celery seed

Combine the vinegar and 1 cup water. Mix the flour, mustard, salt, vinegar mixture, brown sugar and 1 cup cold water. Boil for 15 minutes, stirring constantly. Add the beets and celery seed. Pour into hot sterilized jars and seal while hot.

Mrs. Ethel Benson, Oklahoma City, Oklahoma

BEETS

1 bushel beets without tops   **Salt**

Sort the beets for size. Wash, leaving 2 inches of stems and the top roots. Cover the beets with boiling water and boil until skin slips easily. Remove the skin and trim stems and roots. Leave the small beets whole and cut the large ones in desired shapes. Pack into hot sterilized jars up to 1 inch from top. Add 1 teaspoon salt to each quart, then cover the beets with boiling water, leaving 1 inch head space. Place caps on jars and process for 35 minutes at 10 pounds pressure. About 18 quarts.

Photograph for this recipe on page 32.

BROCCOLI

Broccoli   **Salt**

Wash the broccoli carefully and discard all but the green parts. Cut into 2-inch pieces or larger pieces, as desired. Boil in a small amount of water for 3 minutes, then pack into hot sterilized jars. Add 1 teaspoon salt to each quart and cover with boiling water. Place the lids and bands on the jars and process at 10 pounds pressure for 35 minutes.

Mrs. Laura Baylor, Lexington, Kentucky

CELERY

Celery   **Salt**

Wash and cut the celery in 2-inch pieces. Cover with boiling water and boil for 3 minutes. Pack in hot sterilized jars to 1 inch from tops. Add 1 teaspoon salt to each quart, then cover with water in which celery was boiled. Adjust jar lids. Process for 35 minutes at 10 pounds pressure.

Mrs. E. S. Spencer, Greenville, South Carolina

CARROTS

12 lb. young tender carrots   **Salt**

Scrape the carrots, then slice, dice or leave whole. Place in a large saucepan and cover with boiling water. Boil for 3 minutes, then pack into hot sterilized jars, leaving 1 inch head space. Add 1/2 teaspoon salt to each pint, then cover with boiling water to 1/2 inch from top of jar. Adjust jar lids and process for 25 minutes at 10 pounds pressure.

Mrs. C. H. Crook, Wilson, North Carolina

CAULIFLOWER

Cauliflower   **Salt**

Wash the cauliflower carefully and separate into flowerets. Soak for 10 minutes in salt water, using 1 tablespoon salt per quart water, then drain. Boil for 3 minutes in water to cover. Pack into hot sterilized jars and cover with boiling water. Process pints for 30 minutes and quarts for 35 minutes at 10 pounds pressure. Do not store cauliflower for long periods.

Mrs. Colleen Parks, Guntersville, Alabama

EGGPLANT

Eggplant   **Salt**

Wash and pare the eggplant, then slice or cut in cubes. Sprinkle lightly with salt and cover with water. Soak for 20 minutes, then drain. Boil in a small amount of water for 5 minutes. Pack hot eggplant in hot sterilized jars, leaving 1 inch head space. Add 1 teaspoon salt to each quart. Cover with hot water to within 1 inch of jar top. Adjust jar lids and process for 40 minutes at 10 pounds pressure.

Mrs. Orin Madison, Dover, Delaware

LYE HOMINY

6 c. shelled white or   **1 tsp. concentrated lye**
**   yellow corn**   **Salt**

Combine the corn, lye and 6 cups water in an enameled boiler or a stainless steel kettle and boil for about 25 minutes or until the hulls are loosened. Rinse the corn through several changes of hot water, then cover with cold water. Let stand for 2 to 3 hours, changing water 3 or 4 times to remove all the lye. Rub to remove hulls and black tips. Drain and cover with boiling salted water. Boil until almost tender, then pour immediately into hot sterilized jars. Cover hominy with boiling water, leaving 1 inch head space. Place lids on jars and tighten the rings. Process pints for 1 hour and quarts for 1 hour and 10 minutes at 10 pounds pressure.

Evelyn Bell, Hereford, Texas

GREEN TOMATO SLICES

1 doz. firm green tomatoes	**1/2 c. sugar**
1 tbsp. salt	**1 c. vinegar**

Wash the tomatoes thoroughly and drain. Cut into 1/2-inch slices and sprinkle with the salt. Let stand for 1 hour and drain. Combine the sugar, vinegar and 1 cup water in a saucepan and boil for 5 minutes, stirring until the sugar is dissolved. Pack the tomato slices carefully into hot sterilized jars and cover with the hot vinegar mixture. Fill jars with boiling water, if needed. Process for 20 minutes in boiling water in a waterbath canner.

Mrs. Hallie Slayton, Louisville, Kentucky

CORN AND LIMAS

Fresh corn on the cob	**Salt**
Fresh green lima beans	

Drop the corn in boiling water and boil for 5 minutes. Cool, then cut from cob. Do not scrape. Combine equal amounts of corn and lima beans in large kettle, then add enough water to cover. Bring to a boil. Place in sterilized jars, leaving 1-inch head space. Cover with boiling water, then add 1/2 teaspoon salt to pint jars or 1 teaspoon to quart jars. Seal the jars. Process pint jars for 55 minutes at 10 pounds pressure and quart jars for 1 hour and 25 minutes.

*Tomato Paste (page 40); Corn and Limas (above); Canned Beans (page 42);
Stewed Tomatoes (page 40)*

MARY'S TOMATO MIX

4 green peppers	Salt
1 gal. quartered tomatoes	

Wash and finely chop the peppers. Cook in water to cover until tender. Combine with the tomatoes in a large kettle and simmer until tomatoes are cooked thoroughly. Pack in hot sterilized pint jars and add 1/2 teaspoon salt to each jar. Seal while hot. May be used for meat loaf, chili and spaghetti sauce.

Mrs. Elbert M. Rogers, Camden, Tennessee

TOMATOES AND CELERY

Peeled, cored and chopped tomatoes	Diced celery
	Salt

Combine equal parts tomatoes and celery in a large pot and boil for 5 minutes. Pack immediately into hot sterilized jars, leaving 1 inch head space. Add 1/2 teaspoon salt to each pint jar and 1 teaspoon to each quart, then cover tomato mixture with boiling water to 1 inch from jar top. Place lids on jars and tighten. Process pints for 30 minutes and quarts for 35 minutes at 10 pounds pressure.

Mrs. Joe Huff, Little Rock, Arkansas

TOMATOES AND OKRA

Tomatoes	Sliced okra

Peel, core and chop the tomatoes, then measure. Cook the tomatoes for 20 minutes over low heat. Add an equal amount of sliced okra and boil for 5 minutes, then pour immediately into hot sterilized jars, filling to 1 inch from tops. Add 1 teaspoon salt to each quart and place caps on jars. Process for 35 minutes at 10 pounds pressure.

Mrs. Sylvia Percy, Pass Christian, Mississippi

MIXED VEGETABLE SALAD

1 bunch carrots	3 c. sugar
8 c. green beans	1/4 c. salt
8 c. shelled lima beans	3 tbsp. celery seed
1 lge. head cauliflower	3 tbsp. mustard seed
4 ears of corn	2 tbsp. dry mustard
2 lb. green tomatoes	1 tbsp. turmeric powder
5 green peppers	3 qt. vinegar
2 lb. small white onions	2 tbsp. hot sauce

Pare and slice the carrots, then place the whole green beans, limas and carrot slices in a deep kettle. Break up the cauliflower and cut the corn from the cob, then add to the kettle. Add water to cover and bring to a boil. Reduce heat and cook for 25 minutes, then drain. Coarsely chop tomatoes and green peppers. Peel the onions and set aside. Combine the sugar, salt, celery seed, mustard seed, dry mustard and turmeric in a deep kettle, then add the vinegar. Cook over low heat, stirring constantly, until the sugar is dissolved, then stir in the hot sauce. Add the drained cooked vegetables, chopped vegetables and onions and cook for 25 minutes. Spoon into sterilized jars and seal.

Mixed Vegetable Salad (page 46)

SUCCOTASH

Fresh corn on cob   **Green lima beans, shelled**

Boil the corn in water to cover for 5 minutes. Cut the kernels from the cob, but do not scrape. Boil the lima beans in water to cover for 3 minutes. Measure equal amounts of the corn and lima beans and pack in hot jars, leaving 1 inch space at the top. Add 1 teaspoon salt to each quart and cover with boiling water. Place the lids and rings on the jars. Process for 1 hour and 25 minutes at 10 pounds pressure in a pressure canner.

Mrs. Forrest Maxwell, Gulfport, Mississippi

CREAM-STYLE CORN

Fresh ears of corn   **Salt**

Remove the husks and silk from the ears of corn. Rinse thoroughly. Cut the tip ends from the kernels and scrape out pulp, then measure. Add 1 teaspoon salt and 2 1/2 cups boiling water to each quart of corn, then boil for 3 minutes. Pour immediately into hot pint jars up to 1 inch from tops. Adjust the caps and process for 1 hour and 25 minutes at 10 pounds pressure.

COLD-PACK WHOLE-KERNEL CORN

Pack corn loosely into a hot sterilized jar, leaving 1-inch head space. Do not press down. Add the salt and cover with boiling water, leaving 1 inch space at the top. Place a lid and ring on the jar and tighten. Process at 10 pounds pressure for 1 hour and 25 minutes. Recipe may be increased for larger amount of corn.

RHUBARB

Rhubarb   **Sugar**

Wash rhubarb and cut into 1 1/2-inch pieces. Add 1/2 to 1 cup sugar to each quart rhubarb and let stand to draw out juice. Bring to a boil and pour immediately into hot sterilized jars, leaving 1/2 inch for expansion. Adjust jar lids and place in waterbath canner. Process for 10 minutes at 212 degrees.

Mrs. Natalie Richey, Enid, Oklahoma

MUSHROOMS

Fresh mushrooms   **Ascorbic acid**
Salt

Wash the mushrooms thoroughly and trim. Cover with cold water and let stand for 10 minutes. Drain and wash again. Cook, but do not boil, in just enough water to prevent sticking for 15 minutes. Pack the hot mushrooms into hot sterilized jars, leaving 1 inch for expansion. Add 1/2 teaspoon salt and 1/8 teaspoon ascorbic acid to each pint. Add boiling water to cover the mushrooms, leaving 1 inch head space. Place caps on jars and tighten. Process for 30 minutes at 10 pounds pressure.

Mrs. C. L. Sledge, Knoxville, Tennessee

OKRA

Young, tender okra pods   **Salt**

Leave the okra pods whole for a more attractive finished product. Cook for 1 minute in boiling water and pack immediately into hot sterilized jars, leaving 3/4 inch at the top. Cover the okra with boiling water, leaving at least 1/2 inch head space. Add 1 teaspoon salt to each quart, then place lids and rings in position and tighten. Process in a pressure canner at 10 pounds pressure for 40 minutes.

Mrs. Gordon Phillips, Enid, Oklahoma

PARSNIPS

Small to med. parsnips   **Salt**

Discard the parsnip tops, then wash and peel. Cut into small cubes or slices and cover with boiling water. Bring to a boil, then pack into hot sterilized jars. Add 1 teaspoon salt to each quart, then cover with the boiling blanching water. Adjust the jar lids and rings. Process in a pressure cooker for 40 minutes at 10 pounds pressure.

Mrs. Dixie Lewis, Columbus, Georgia

PECANS

4 pt. shelled pecans

Place the pecans in a shallow pan. Bake at 250 degrees until dry. Boil the canning jars for 5 minutes, then invert on a clean cloth to drain. Pack the hot pecans into dry jars and adjust the lids. Process for 10 minutes at 5 pounds pressure.

Mrs. Willa Martin, Montgomery, Alabama

GREEN PEAS

Young tender peas   **Salt**

Too mature peas will not give a pleasing green product. Select only the freshly gathered young peas to can. Shell, then cover with boiling water and bring to a boil. Pack loosely in hot jars and cover with the blanching water, leaving 1/2 inch head space. Add 1 teaspoon salt to each quart. Place the lids and rings on the jars and tighten. Process in a pressure canner for 40 minutes at 10 pounds pressure.

Mrs. Evelyn Rogers, Columbus, Mississippi

BLACK-EYED PEAS

Black-eyed peas   **Salt**

Wash and shell the peas, then cover with boiling water and bring to a boil. Cook for about 5 minutes. Pack into hot sterilized jars to 1 1/2 inches from tops. Add 1 teaspoon salt to each quart jar, then cover with boiling liquid, leaving at least 1/2 inch head space. Adjust the caps and process at 10 pounds pressure for 40 minutes in a pressure canner.

Mrs. Opal Davis, Waco, Texas

POTATOES

Salt   **Potatoes**

Combine 1 teaspoon salt and 1 quart water to make a brine. Prepare in proportion to amount of potatoes. Wash, peel and cut the potatoes in 1/2 inch cubes. Drop in the prepared brine to prevent darkening, then drain. Cook for 2 minutes in boiling water and drain. Pack immediately in hot jars, leaving 1/2 inch head space. Add 1 teaspoon salt to each quart and cover with boiling water. Adjust the jar lids. Process in a pressure canner at 10 pounds pressure for 40 minutes.

Mrs. Coleta Chrisman, Yuma, Arizona

PUMPKIN

Pumpkins   **Salt**

Wash the pumpkins and cut in sections for easier handling. Peel and cut into 1-inch cubes. Add just enough water to cover, then bring to a boil. Pack immediately in hot jars, leaving 3/4 inch head space, and cover with the hot cooking liquid. Add 1 teaspoon salt to each quart and work out any air bubbles with a knife blade. Place the lids on the jars and screw on the rings. Process at 10 pounds pressure in a pressure canner for 1 hour and 30 minutes.

Mrs. Mary Bruner, Samson, Alabama

SPINACH

Freshly picked, tender spinach   **Salt**

Inspect the spinach carefully and remove any imperfections, then wash thoroughly. Cut out stems and midribs, then wash the leaves carefully in running water. Cover the spinach with hot, not boiling, water and cook, uncovered, for about 5 minutes or until wilted. Pack loosely to within 3/4 inch of jar top and cover with boiling water, leaving 1/2 inch head space. Add 1 teaspoon salt to each quart. Place caps on jars and tighten. Process at 10 pounds pressure in a pressure canner for 1 hour and 30 minutes.

Mrs. James L. Ashburn, Little Rock, Arkansas

SUMMER SQUASH

Squash   **Salt**

Wash the squash with a vegetable brush, then cut into cubes. Cover with boiling water and bring again to a boil. Pack into hot jars and leave 1/2 inch at the top. Cover with hot liquid and add 1 teaspoon salt to each quart. Adjust the jar lids and process for 40 minutes at 10 pounds pressure in a pressure canner.

Mrs. Nancy Todd, New Orleans, Louisiana

SWEET POTATOES

Sweet potatoes   **Medium syrup**
Salt

Wash the sweet potatoes and sort for size. Boil in water to cover just until peel slips easily. Remove the peel and cut in large chunks. Pack the hot sweet potatoes in hot jars to 1 inch from the top. Add 1 teaspoon salt to each quart, then cover with boiling syrup. Adjust jar lids and rings. Process at 10 pounds pressure in a pressure canner for 1 hour and 30 minutes.

Mrs. Annie M. Monroe, Greenwood, Mississippi

SALSIFY

Freshly dug salsify   **Vinegar**

Wash the salsify thoroughly. Prepare vinegar water in porportion to amount of salsify, using 1 tablespoon vinegar to each quart of water. Boil the salsify in the vinegar water for 15 minutes, then rinse in cool water. Scrape to remove the peel. Slice large salsify, if desired. Pack into hot jars, leaving 1 inch space at top of jars. Place the lids and rings on the jars and tighten. Process at 10 pounds pressure in a pressure canner for 35 minutes.

Mrs. C. Carroll Buchanan, Wheaton, Maryland

SOYBEANS

Green soybeans   **Salt**

Wash, drain and shell the soybeans, then rinse. Place in a saucepan with a small amount of water, then bring to a boil and boil for 3 minutes. Pack immediately in hot sterilized jars. Add 1 teaspoon salt to each quart or 1/2 teaspoon to each pint. Cover with boiling water. Process at 10 pounds pressure for 1 hour and 20 minutes.

Mrs. Beryl Nixon, Covington, Kentucky

meats, poultry, and seafood

Have you ever been confronted with a wonderfully inexpensive special on meat, poultry, or seafood . . . a fisherman's or hunter's huge catch . . . or some other plentiful supply of food you wished you could keep? *Southern Living* homemakers have — and they have developed perfect preserving recipes so that they *can* take advantage of all kinds of low-cost bargains.

As you turn through these pages, you find recipes telling you how to preserve fish . . . shellfish . . . chicken . . . quail . . . beef . . . pork . . . mincemeat . . . and more. Some of the recipes are for combination dishes, like Chile Con Carne with Baked Beans. Just imagine being able to treat your husband and children to this hearty dish — prepared and preserved by you. Or picture yourself serving Chicken a la King at a hurry-up party meal — using food you have preserved months in advance. You'll delight in an old-time recipe for Brunswick Stew, so chock full of chicken, beef, pork, and succulent vegetables, it'll be everyone's favorite.

Accompanying the recipes are pages of the latest, most accurate information on the best and safest way to preserve meat, fish, and seafood. It tells you in graphic detail what to do and what not to do so that your family can enjoy fresh-tasting foods year-round, foods with just-prepared flavor and all the economy of canning. For delicious-tasting family-approved recipes, depend on this section every time!

53

Before beginning your preparations, you may want to review *Correct Procedure* under "Successful Canning and Preserving" on pages 9 and 10. Detailed information on preparing meat, poultry, or seafood for canning is given in the section below and in the specific recipes. When canning meats, poultry, and seafood, *always* follow the recipe instructions closely and adhere accurately to the time alloted for processing.

For beef, veal, pork, lamb, and large game . . .

1. Choose clean, fresh, well bled meat. Chill thoroughly: pork, lamb, and veal, 24 to 36 hours; beef and large game, 36 to 48 hours. Avoid

canning
instructions

FOR MEATS, POULTRY, AND SEAFOOD

freezing. Frozen meat is difficult to handle and yields a canned product of poor quality.

2. Wipe the meat with a clean damp cloth. Do not wash; washing draws out valuable juices. For some strong-flavored game, soaking in salt water is recommended.

3. Cut the meat into pieces suitable for cooking or canning. Cut slices across the grain about 1 inch thick; cut jar-sized pieces and chunks with the grain. To can large pieces of meat, select the finer cuts. For stew meat use the smaller less tender cuts.

4. Bone the meat and trim away gristle, bruised areas, and fat. Too much fat is likely to cause a strong, unpleasant flavor in the canned product. It may also ruin the rubber used to seal the jar.

> NOTE: In most states the length of time that canned game animals can be safely stored is controlled by law. Conservation officials can supply information on this subject.

For poultry, game birds, and rabbit . . .

1. Select only healthy, plump poultry. One or two year old fowls are better for canning than younger birds. Chill the poultry for 6 to 12 hours. Avoid freezing.

2. Wipe the poultry thoroughly with a clean damp cloth.

3. Cut the poultry into pieces suitable for cooking or canning. Remove the

giblets; they should be canned separately. Separate the meaty pieces from the bony ones.

4. Simmer the bony pieces in water to cover until the meat is tender and the broth is flavored. Skim the broth. You will use this broth to fill the canning jars after the poultry has been packed inside.

5. Trim away the large lumps of fat from the meaty pieces. Poultry may be packed with or without the bones. You may bone your poultry raw or after precooking.

For fish and shellfish . . .

1. Can only freshly caught fish and shellfish. Fish should be thoroughly bled. Pack the seafood on ice until you are ready to begin preparations for canning.

2. For fish, remove the scales, fins, and head, but not backbone. Remove the entrails. Wash in cool water. For shellfish, prepare according to the recipe instructions. This usually involves steaming the shellfish in order to remove the meat.

3. Cut the seafood into jar-sized pieces. If specified in your recipe, soak or dip the seafood in brine for the recommended length of time.

NOTE: Do not attempt to reprocess seafood products that do not seal properly during processing.

Certain fish are unsuitable for canning. The Division of Fishery Industries, United States Department of Agriculture, is supplied with this detailed information.

GENERAL DIRECTIONS

After you have prepared your food for canning, follow the general directions given below and your specific recipe instructions for packing and processing. These steps apply to meat, poultry, and seafood.

1. Use the hot or raw pack procedure specified in the particular recipe that you are following. Leave about 1 inch head space.
2. Cover the food with hot liquid, again leaving 1 inch head space.
3. Work out air bubbles with a knife. Add more liquid if needed.
4. Wipe jar tops and threads with a clean, damp cloth before capping.
5. Adjust the lids on the canning jars.
6. Review the instructions on how to operate a pressure canner found either on pages 8 to 9 or 34 to 36.
7. Process in pressure canner at 10 pounds pressure (240 degrees). For meat and poultry (without bone) — Pint jars — 75 minutes processing time. Quart jars — 90 minutes processing time.
    For meat and poultry (with bone) — Pint jars — 65 minutes processing time. Quart jars — 75 minutes processing time.
    For fish and shellfish — See specific recipes.

CORNED BEEF

25 lb. beef brisket   **1 1/2 tsp. soda**
2 lb. pickling salt   **1 oz. saltpeter**
1 lb. sugar

Cut the beef into 3 to 6-inch thick pieces. Pour a thin layer of salt in the bottom of a stone jar or a tight wooden keg. Add layers of beef and salt, ending with salt until all the beef is used. Let stand overnight. Dissolve the sugar, soda and saltpeter in 1 quart lukewarm water, then mix with 3 quarts tap water and pour over the beef. Cover with a glass pie plate and a weight to hold the plate below the brine. Remove scum each day. The beef is ready to can when a bright red color develops. Wash the corned beef and cut into desired lengths. Cover with cold water and bring to a boil. Taste the broth and drain if too salty, then cover again with cold water. Bring to a boil and pack immediately into hot jars, leaving 1 inch head space. Cover the corned beef with the hot broth or boiling water and place the lids and rings on the jars. Process in a pressure canner at 10 pounds pressure for 1 hour and 30 minutes for quarts.

Mrs. Dora Steele, Oklahoma City, Oklahoma

BEEF PATTIES

4 lb. lean ground beef   **4 tsp. salt**

Mix the ground beef and salt well, then press into thin patties which can be packed in jars without breaking. Place the patties on a greased shallow baking pan. Bake at 350 degrees for about 30 minutes or until any red color has disappeared. Pack the hot patties in wide-mouthed jars. Skim the fat from the baking pan and add hot water to the pan. Bring to a boil, stirring, over medium heat. Pour the hot liquid over the patties, allowing 1 inch at the top for expansion. Adjust the lids and process at 10 pounds pressure for 1 hour and 15 minutes. About 4 pints.

Mrs. Rose Payne, Bay St. Louis, Mississippi

BEEF RUMP ROAST

5 lb. beef rump roast   **Salt**

Cut the beef away from the bone and reserve the bones to make stock. Trim away most of the fat and cut the beef in large chunks. Place the beef chunks in a large kettle and add a small amount of water. Cover and cook over low heat, turning occasionally, until the beef is about medium done. Add 1 teaspoon salt to each quart jar for flavor, if desired. Pack the hot beef in the jars, leaving 1 inch for expansion. Cover with the juice in which the beef was cooked, adding hot broth or water, if needed. Adjust the lids and process in a pressure canner at 10 pounds pressure for 1 hour and 30 minutes.

Beef Rump Roast (page 56)

BEEF STEW

5 lb. (about) beef stew meat	3 c. chopped celery
2 qt. sliced carrots	1 1/2 tbsp. salt
3 qt. pared, cubed potatoes	1 tsp. thyme
3 c. chopped onions	1/2 tsp. pepper

Cut the beef in 1 1/2-inch cubes and brown in a small amount of fat. Combine the beef, vegetables and seasonings in a large kettle and cover with boiling water. Pack into hot jars to 1 inch from top and place lids and rings on the jars. Process at 10 pounds pressure for 1 hour and 15 minutes for quart jars.

Mrs. Juanita Foster, Fort Worth, Texas

CHILI CON CARNE WITH BAKED BEANS

4 onions, diced	6 c. cooked red kidney beans
1/4 c. shortening	1 1/2 tsp. chili powder
1 qt. chopped tomatoes	1 tbsp. salt
4 lb. ground beef	

Cook the onions in hot fat in a skillet until golden brown, then remove from the skillet and drain. Combine the onions and remaining ingredients in a large kettle and bring to a boil, stirring constantly. Ladle the hot mixture into hot sterilized jars. Place the caps and rings on the jars and tighten. Process at 10 pounds pressure for 1 hour and 15 minutes for pint jars.

Mrs. Anne Bailey, Nashville, Tennessee

CHILI

5 lb. ground beef	1/2 c. chili powder
2 c. chopped onions	1 1/2 tbsp. salt
1 garlic clove, minced	1 hot red pepper
6 c. cooked tomatoes	1 tsp. cumin seed

Brown the ground beef in a skillet, then add the onions and garlic and cook over low heat until just tender. Add the remaining ingredients and simmer for 15 minutes. Skim off excess fat, then pour the hot mixture into hot quart jars, allowing 1 inch for head space. Position the jar caps and tighten. Process in a pressure canner at 10 pounds pressure for 1 hour and 30 minutes. Add cooked or canned pinto beans to chili mixture, then bring to a boil and cook until heated through.

Mrs. Rosa Perrini, Santa Fe, New Mexico

MINCEMEAT

4 lb. beef, diced	2 lb. sugar
2 lb. beef suet	1 nutmeg, grated

1 tbsp. cloves	1/2 lb. candied lemon peel,
1 tbsp. cinnamon	minced
1 tsp. salt	Grated rind of 2 oranges
2 lb. seedless raisins, chopped	Grated rind of 1 lemon
2 lb. currants	1/2 c. orange juice
4 lb. apples, finely chopped	1/2 c. lemon juice
1/2 lb. citron, minced	4 c. hard cider

Boil the meat and suet in a small amount of water until tender, then drain and cool. Force the beef and suet through a food chopper and combine with remaining ingredients. Cook, covered, for 1 hour. Pour into hot sterilized jars and adjust the lids. Process at 10 pounds pressure for 30 minutes. Brandy to taste may be added to canned mincemeat before using for pie filling.

Mrs. Nell Skinner, Nashville, Tennessee

LIVER PASTE

3 lb. liver	2 tsp. salt
1/4 lb. salt pork, sliced	1/4 tsp. dry mustard
1 med. onion	1/4 tsp. hot sauce
1/4 c. catsup	2 c. meat stock

Cook the liver and salt pork in a small amount of water until tender and drain. Chop the liver mixture and onion with the fine blade of a food chopper. Add the catsup, seasonings, hot sauce and meat stock to make a smooth paste. Cook until heated through. Pack immediately into hot jars, leaving 1 inch for head space. Fit jars with lids and process half-pints for 1 hour and 25 minutes or pints for 1 hour and 30 minutes at 10 pounds pressure. Canned liver paste may be mixed with mayonnaise or sour cream before using for a sandwich spread or appetizer.

Mrs. Ethel Clements, Lawton, Oklahoma

CANNED PORK CHOPS

Pork chops	1 tsp. salt

Cut the meat away from the bones, then cut in cubes. Leave a small amount of fat on the pork. Pack the pork into sterilized jars and add 1 teaspoon salt to each quart jar. Set the open jars in a large kettle containing warm water to within 2 inches from the tops of the jars. Cover the kettle and bring the water to the simmering point. Cook for about 1 hour and 15 minutes or until medium done. Add boiling water to the jars, if needed, to cover the pork and leave 1 inch head space. Place the caps on the jars and process at 10 pounds pressure for 1 hour and 30 minutes. 4-6 servings per quart jar.

Mrs. Tally Alexander, Puryear, Tennessee

GROUND PORK

5 lb. ground pork   **1 tbsp. salt**
3 c. (about) tomato juice

Have the butcher grind the lean pork or put through a home grinder. Brown the ground pork, stirring constantly, over high heat. Combine the pork, juice and salt and pack into hot quart jars, leaving 1 inch head space. Process for 1 hour and 30 minutes at 10 pounds pressure. Canned ground pork may be used for stuffing vegetables or in combination with other ground meat for meat loaves.

Mrs. George Weathers, Greensboro, North Carolina

SPARERIBS

Spareribs   **Salt**

Crack the spareribs evenly. Cook in water to cover until about half done, then cut into squares and remove the bones. Sprinkle with salt and pack into hot quart jars to within 1 inch from top. Cover with the hot broth, leaving 1 inch head space. Place the caps on the jars and tighten. Process at 10 pounds pressure for 1 hour and 30 minutes. Canned spareribs may be covered with barbecue sauce and cooked until heated through.

Mrs. Louise Long, Cleveland, Mississippi

CHICKEN A LA KING

8 lb. stewing chicken pieces	**Salt**
2 stalks celery	**1/2 c. flour**
1 onion	**5 c. chicken broth**
1 carrot	**1/2 c. chopped celery**
4 peppercorns	**1/4 c. chopped pimento**
2 whole allspice	**1 tbsp. chopped parsley**
1 bay leaf	**Pepper to taste**

Place the chicken in water to cover in a large kettle. Add the celery, onion, carrot, peppercorns, allspice, bay leaf and 2 teaspoons salt. Bring to a boil and reduce the heat, then simmer for about 2 hours or until the chicken is tender. Remove the vegetables, spices and bay leaf. Allow the chicken pieces to cool in the broth, then remove from broth. Spoon off the excess fat, reserving 1/4 cup, and strain the broth. Remove the skin and bones from the chicken and cut the meat into chunks. Melt the reserved chicken fat in a large saucepan. Add the flour and stir until smooth. Add the chicken broth gradually and cook, stirring constantly, until thickened. Add the chicken, chopped ingredients and pepper and simmer for 5 minutes. Pack into hot pint jars, leaving 1 inch space at the top. Adjust the lids and process for 1 hour and 5 minutes. Other ingredients to suit individual tastes may be added to Chicken A La King before serving.

Mrs. James Washburn, Greenwood, Mississippi

COLD PACK CHICKEN WITH BONES

4 chickens, disjointed   **Salt**

Trim off large lumps of fat from the chicken and sort into meaty pieces and bony pieces. Can giblets separately. Remove the breast bone and saw off the small end of the drumsticks, if desired. Leave the bones in remaining pieces. Measure 1/2 teaspoon salt in pint jars and 1 teaspoon salt in quart jars. Pack the second joints and drumsticks with the skin next to the glass. Place the breasts in the center and slip in smaller pieces to fit. Leave 1 inch at the top of the jars and add no liquid. Set the open jars in a large container, such as a waterbath canner, and add warm water to about 2 inches from rim of jars. Cover the container, and boil over low heat for about 1 hour and 15 minutes or until all the chicken is medium done. Adjust the jar lids and process in a pressure canner at 10 pounds pressure for 1 hour and 5 minutes.

Photograph for this recipe on page 52.

CHICKEN WITH DUMPLINGS

2 4-lb. stewing hens	**2 med. onions, sliced**
4 tsp. salt	**3 whole cloves**
1/2 tsp. pepper	**1 recipe dumplings**
2 c. diced celery	

Place the hens in 4 cups water in a large kettle and add the salt, pepper, celery, onions and cloves. Bring to a boil and cover, then reduce the heat. Simmer for about 1 hour or until the hens are tender. Remove and discard the skin and bones, then cut the chicken in bite-sized pieces. Strain the broth into a large kettle and add the chicken pieces. Roll out the dumpling dough and cut in 2-inch strips. Drop the dumplings into the broth and bring to a boil. Spoon immediately into hot sterilized pint jars. Place the lids and rings on the jars and tighten. Process at 10 pounds pressure for 1 hour.

Mrs. Sara Lewis, Atlanta, Georgia

CHICKEN SPREAD FOR SANDWICHES

8 lb. cut-up chicken	**Salt**
1 bunch celery	**1/4 c. mustard**
2 onions	**1 tbsp. grated onion**
1 carrot	**1 tbsp. vinegar**
4 peppercorns	**Pepper to taste**
1 bay leaf	

Combine the chicken, water to cover, celery, onions, carrot, peppercorns, bay leaf and 2 teaspoons salt in a large kettle and bring to a boil. Cover and reduce heat, then simmer for about 2 hours or until the chicken is tender. Remove the vegetables, then cool and chill the chicken and broth. Skim off the fat, then reserve 1 cup broth. Remove and discard the skin and bones from the chicken, then grind the meat. Combine the ground chicken, reserved broth and remaining ingredients. Pack into hot half-pint jars, leaving 1 inch head space. Place the caps on the jars. Process for 1 hour at 10 pounds pressure.

Mrs. Lynn Madison, Huntsville, Alabama

BONED CHICKEN

8 lb. chicken   Salt

Boil the chicken in water to cover until almost done and remove the skin and bones. Pack the meat into hot sterilized jars and add 1/2 teaspoon salt to each pint and 1 teaspoon salt to each quart. Skim the fat from the broth and bring the broth to a boil. Pour over the chicken, leaving 1 inch at the top. Fit lids on the jars and tighten the rings. Process pints for 1 hour and 15 minutes and quarts for 1 hour and 30 minutes at 10 pounds pressure.

Mrs. Grady Ames, Sumter, South Carolina

CANNED QUAIL IN SHERRY

6 quail, dressed   1/4 c. finely chopped celery
1/2 c. chopped salt pork   Sherry
1 sm. carrot, finely chopped   6 peppercorns
1 onion, chopped   1/2 tsp. salt

Wipe the quail thoroughly. Place the salt pork, carrot, onion and celery in a heavy kettle or Dutch oven. Arrange the quail over the vegetable mixture and add just enough sherry to cover. Add the peppercorns and salt and bring to a boil. Cover. Bake at 375 degrees for 35 minutes. Pack 2 quail in each of 3 quart jars. Strain the cooking liquid and pour over the quail to cover, leaving 1 inch head space. Fit the jars with lids and process at 10 pounds pressure for 1 hour and 15 minutes.

Mrs. Harry Foshee, Wilmington, North Carolina

ROAST TURKEY

2 sm. turkeys   Salt

Bake the turkeys at 300 degrees until almost done. Cut the meat from the bones and pack into hot jars. Add 1 teaspoon salt to each quart and cover with hot broth, leaving 1 inch at the top for expansion. Adjust the jar caps and process at 10 pounds pressure for 1 hour and 30 minutes. Canned turkey may be used for casseroles, loaves or barbecued for sandwiches.

Mrs. Cora Springfield, Oklahoma City, Oklahoma

BRUNSWICK STEW

1 6-lb. baking hen   2 qt. tomatoes
2 1/2 lb. stew beef   2 pt. tomato soup
1 2 1/2-lb. fresh pork roast   1/2 lb. margarine
1 lb. dried lima beans   1 can tomato paste
5 lb. onions   Salt and pepper to taste
10 lb. potatoes   1 pod red pepper

Boil the hen, the stew beef and the pork roast separately in water to cover, then chop. Reserve the broth. Soak the beans in water to cover overnight, then drain. Cook the beans in meat broth to cover until just tender. Peel the onions and potatoes and cut in cubes. Combine the chopped meats, the vegetables and remaining ingredients in a large kettle and bring to a boil. Pack in quart jars. Skim the fat off the reserved broth and bring to a boil. Fill the jars with broth to within 1 inch of the tops. Place lids and rings on the jars and process at 10 pounds pressure for 1 hour and 30 minutes.

Mrs. Theda Steele, Richmond, Virginia

COLD-PACK RABBIT

Salt   **Rabbits, dressed and disjointed**

Dissolve 1 tablespoon salt in 1 quart water in amount needed to soak the rabbits, then soak for 1 hour. Rinse and pack into hot sterilized jars, leaving 1 inch head space. Adjust caps on the jars and process pints for 1 hour and 5 minutes and quarts for 1 hour and 15 minutes at 10 pounds pressure.

Mrs. Loraine Langley, Pine Bluff, Arkansas

COD

Salt   **Fresh cod**

Make a brine by dissolving 1 cup salt in 1 gallon water. Clean the cod and wash thoroughly, then cut into large chunks. Soak the chunks in the brine for about 1 hour, then rinse and drain. Place the cod on racks or pans with perforated bottoms and stack in a pressure cooker with about 3 inches of water in the bottom. Cook at 10 pounds pressure for 30 minutes, then cool. Remove the skin and bones and discard. Discard any discolored meat, also. Pack the remaining meat in pint jars and remove any air bubbles with a knife blade. Adjust the jar caps and process at 10 pounds pressure for 1 hour and 40 minutes.

Mrs. Bobby Cox, Baltimore, Maryland

TROUT

Salt   **Cleaned trout**

Dissolve 1 cup salt in 1 gallon water for brine. Cut the trout in lengths to fit the canning jars. Soak the trout for 1 hour in the brine, then drain. Pack in hot pint jars with the skin next to the glass, leaving 1 inch head space. Combine 1/2 cup salt and 1 gallon water and heat, stirring, until dissolved. Place the open jars in a kettle and cover with the hot brine. Boil for 15 minutes. Remove the jars and invert to drain, then place the caps on the jars. Process for 1 hour and 40 minutes at 10 pounds pressure.

Mrs. Jackie Myers, Laurel, Mississippi

SMELT IN BARBECUE SAUCE

6 lb. smelt, cleaned	1/4 c. vinegar
2 c. barbecue sauce	2 tsp. salt
3/4 c. salad oil	

Pack the smelt into hot pint jars, leaving 1 inch head space. Combine the remaining ingredients and pour over the smelt, adding water, if needed, to cover. Place the lids and rings on the jars and tighten. Process for 50 minutes at 10 pounds pressure. Barbecue sauce may be a favorite homemade recipe.

Mrs. S. A. Parrish, Dover, Delaware

TUNA

Tuna	Salt

Clean the tuna thoroughly and rinse carefully in cold water. Place the tuna in a wire basket or in pans with perforated bottoms and lower in a pressure cooker containing about 3 inches of hot water. Cook the tuna at 10 pounds pressure for 2 hours, then cool and chill for about 6 hours. Cut into jar-length pieces and pack into hot pint jars, leaving 1 inch at the top. Add 1 teaspoon salt and 2 tablespoons vegetable oil to each jar and adjust the caps. Process at 10 pounds pressure for 1 hour and 30 minutes.

Mrs. Jeff Kelly, Pensacola, Florida

CLAMS

Clams	Cornmeal
Salt	

Scrub the clams thoroughly. Prepare a brine using about 1 1/2 cups salt per gallon of water and drop the clams in the brine. Add 1 to 2 cups cornmeal and leave the clams to soak for 12 to 24 hours. Open the live clams over a pan and reserve the juice. Open the body of each clam and scrape out the dark mass. Wash the clams through several changes of water. Prepare an acid brine of 1/4 cup vinegar and 1 cup salt to 1 gallon boiling water. Boil the clams for 20 minutes in the acid brine and drain. Remove the meat from the body of each clam. Prepare a cool brine of 1 cup salt, 2 cups white vinegar to 1 gallon water and rinse the clam meat. Squeeze the meat to remove some of the liquid. Pack about 1 3/4 cups clam meat into each pint jar. Add boiling water to the reserved clam juice and strain, then pour over the clam meat to within 1 inch of the top. Adjust the lids and process at 10 pounds pressure for 1 hour and 30 minutes.

Mrs. Frances Lynch, Dundalk, Maryland

LOBSTERS

Live lobsters	Lemon juice
Salt	

Plunge the lobsters into boiling water containing 2 tablespoons salt per gallon of water. Bring again to a boil and cook for 15 to 30 minutes, depending on the size of the lobsters. Cool the lobsters in cold water containing 1 tablespoon salt per gallon. Split the lobsters lengthwise and discard the black veins in the tails and the small sacs just below the heads. Remove the edible meat in large pieces. Crack the claws and remove the meat. Wash in running water and drain thoroughly. Make a solution of 2 quarts water and 1/4 cup lemon juice and dip the meat in the solution. Squeeze the meat to remove any excess moisture. Pack about 3/4 cup lobster meat in half-pint jars, placing the tail meat on the bottom and the claw meat on top. Dissolve 3 tablespoons salt in 1 gallon water and bring to a boil, then pour over the lobster meat. Cover the jars with lids and screw on the rings. Process at 10 pounds pressure for 1 hour and 10 minutes.

Mrs. Nancy Thiessen, Baltimore, Maryland

OYSTERS

Salt   **Oysters**

Prepare a weak brine by dissolving 1/4 cup salt in each gallon of water. Wash the oysters thoroughly in the brine and drain. Pour about 3 inches water in a deep cooker and bring to a boil. Place the oysters in a metal basket and lower into the cooker, then cover. Steam the oysters for 10 to 15 minutes. Shuck the oysters, dropping them into a weak brine to prevent discoloration, then wash them thoroughly in a large quantity of weak brine and drain. Pack about 2 cups oysters into each pint jar and pour in a small amount of weak brine. Cover with lids and screw on the rings. Process for 1 hour and 20 minutes at 10 pounds pressure.

Mrs. Daniel Cowley, Wheaton, Maryland

SHRIMP

Salt   **Shrimp**
Vinegar

Prepare a brine of 1 cup salt and 1 cup vinegar per gallon boiling water. Wash and drain freshly caught shrimp and drop into the boiling brine. Boil for 10 minutes, then drop into cold water. Drain and peel, removing the black vein that runs along the back of the shrimp. Rinse in fresh cool water. Pack into hot pint jars, leaving 1 inch head space, and cover with boiling water. Place the lids and rings on the jars and tighten. Process for 1 hour and 30 minutes at 10 pounds pressure.

Mrs. Patsy Buford, Biloxi, Mississippi

HARD-SHELLED CRABS

6 live crabs   **Salt**

Drop the live crabs, one at a time, into boiling salted water to cover. Bring the water to a boil after each crab is added. Cook for 20 to 25 minutes, then drain and rinse. Break off the claws. Remove the top shell from the tail end. Discard the spongy white fibers and the undershell. Crack the claws and remove the meat. Pack the crab meat from the body and the claws loosely into half-pint or pint jars. Place the lids on the jars and tighten. Process at 10 pounds pressure for 1 hour and 30 minutes.

Mrs. Margaret Harris, Dover, Delaware

Bigos (page 68)

soups
and sauces

Every homemaker knows how easy it is to open a can of soup or sauce and use it as the basis of an in-a-hurry meal. But can you picture how proud you'll feel when the can you open is one you preserved yourself? Southern women prepare huge pots of soup and sauces, serve part of their creation for that evening's meal, and preserve the rest for use throughout the year.

Many of the recipes they use to prepare soups and sauces are now shared with you in the pages that follow. If it's soup you want to prepare, consider the possibilities of preserving your own rich beef Consomme . . . flavorful Pepper Pot Soup . . . or Old-Fashioned Beef with Vegetable Soup, a hearty blend of beef, carrots, tomatoes, and seasonings. With a shelf full of homemade, preserved soups, you'll be able to prepare quick lunches and suppers anytime — for just pennies a serving.

And the sauce recipes! With the home-tested recipes in the pages that follow, you'll have shelves full of zesty, tomato-based Italian Spaghetti Sauce . . . Barbecue Sauce made the hot and spicy southern way . . . palate-tingling Chili Sauce . . . thick tomato Catsup . . . Cranberry Sauce ready for holiday dining . . . and many more.

For years, these recipes have stocked the shelves of families throughout the Southland. Use them now to stock your shelves with soups and sauces you'll depend on year-round for delicious taste.

BIGOS

4 slices bacon, diced	2 tbsp. brown sugar
1 c. chopped onions	3 tbsp. chopped parsley
1/2 lb. sliced mushrooms	1/2 c. water
7 c. undrained sauerkraut	1/2 c. cranberry juice
1 lb. knockwurst, sliced	cocktail
4 c. diced cooked ham	1 10 1/2-oz. can beef
1 med. cored apple, diced	gravy

Combine the bacon, onions and mushrooms in large kettle and cook over medium heat until onions are tender. Add the sauerkraut, knockwurst, ham, apple, sugar and parsley and mix well. Cover and cook over medium heat for 30 minutes, stirring occasionally. Add water, cranberry juice cocktail and gravy. Cook, covered, over low heat for 1 hour, stirring occasionally. Place in hot sterilized jars, leaving 1-inch head space and seal. Process pints for 1 hour and 15 minutes and quarts for 1 hour and 30 minutes at 10 pounds pressure.

Photograph for this recipe on page 66.

CONSOMME

1 lb. lean beef, cubed	1 tbsp. diced celery
1 veal knuckle	1 tbsp. diced carrots
2 peppercorns	1 tbsp. diced onion
1 clove	1 sprig of parsley
1/2 tsp. sweet herbs	1 tsp. salt

Combine the beef cubes, veal knuckle, 1 1/2 quarts water and remaining ingredients in a large kettle and simmer for about 3 hours. Strain through several thicknesses of cheesecloth and cool quickly, then skim off the fat. Pour into pint jars and process for 1 hour at 10 pounds pressure. Canned consomme may be served with shredded chicken and green peas or julienne vegetables or claret.

Mrs. E. B. Draper, Bowling Green, Kentucky

HEARTY HAMBURGER SOUP

2 lge. onions, coarsely chopped	2 bay leaves
1/4 c. melted margarine	1/4 c. chopped celery tops
3 lb. ground beef	6 sprigs of parsley
1 qt. beef stock	1 tsp. thyme
1 qt. canned tomatoes	10 peppercorns
4 carrots, quartered	1 tbsp. salt

Saute the onions in the margarine until limp, then add the ground beef and brown slightly. Stir in remaining ingredients and bring to a boil. Pour into hot jars and adjust the caps. Process at 10 pounds pressure for 1 hour for pints or for 1 hour and 15 minutes for quarts. Discard the bay leaves and peppercorns before serving. Cooked rice may be added to stretch the soup, if desired.

Mrs. J. C. Acker, Birmingham, Alabama

LIVER SOUP

1 lb. beef liver	2 tsp. salt
2 c. chopped mushrooms	6 c. beef stock
4 tsp. minced parsley	2 tbsp. flour
6 tbsp. fat	

Cut the liver into fine pieces, then saute with the mushrooms and parsley in about 4 tablespoons fat for 5 minutes. Add the salt and beef stock and simmer, covered, for 30 minutes or until the liver is tender. Combine the remaining fat and flour and brown, then add the liver mixture. Bring to a boil and pour into hot sterilized jars. Adjust the jar caps and process for 1 hour and 15 minutes at 10 pounds pressure. Add cream or milk for desired consistency, then bring to simmering point and serve.

Mrs. J. C. Bridges, Enid, Oklahoma

VEGETABLE SOUP MIX

1 1/2 qt. water	4 c. cut corn, uncooked
8 c. peeled, cored, chopped	6 c. sliced carrots
tomatoes	2 c. sliced celery
6 c. peeled, cubed potatoes	2 c. chopped onion
4 c. lima beans	Salt

Combine the water and vegetables and boil for 5 minutes. Pour into hot jars, leaving 1-inch headspace. Add 1/4 teaspoon salt to pints and 1/2 teaspoon to quarts. Adjust lids, then process in pressure canner at 10 pounds pressure (240 degrees). Process pints for 55 minutes and quarts for 85 minutes. About 14 pints or 7 quarts.

Photograph for this recipe on page 39.

OLD-FASHIONED BEEF WITH VEGETABLE SOUP

1 2-lb. meaty beef shank bone	2 c. sliced carrots
1 tbsp. salt	1 qt. chopped tomatoes
1/4 tsp. pepper	2 tbsp. chopped parsley
1 1/2 c. chopped onion	1 tsp. basil
1/2 c. barley	

Combine the shank bone, 3 quarts water, salt and pepper in a large kettle and bring to a boil. Simmer for 3 hours, then remove the bone and add the remaining ingredients. Bring to a boil and pour immediately into hot sterilized pint jars. Place lids and rings on the jars and tighten. Process for 1 hour and 15 minutes at 10 pounds pressure in a pressure cooker. Cooked macaroni may be added to the canned soup. Bring to a boil and simmer for 5 minutes, then serve.

Mrs. Joan Thomson, Cordell, Oklahoma

CHICKEN SOUP

2 5-lb. chickens	1 bay leaf
1 med. onion	4 peppercorns
1 med. carrot	4 whole allspice
1/2 c. celery leaves	Salt

Cut the chickens into pieces, reserving the breasts for canning separately. Cover the chicken with water and add the vegetables and spices. Bring to a boil and reduce the heat. Simmer for 2 to 3 hours or until tender. Remove the skin and bones and discard, then cut the meat into small pieces. Strain the broth, skimming off the fat. Add the chicken to the broth, then salt to taste. Boil for 3 minutes and pour immediately into hot sterilized jars, leaving 1 inch at the top of the jars. Place the lids on the jars and tighten the rings. Process pints for 30 minutes and quarts for 45 minutes at 10 pounds pressure. Chicken soup may be heated and served or noodles, macaroni or rice may be added for variety.

Mrs. Virginia C. Smith, Decatur, Georgia

TURKEY SOUP

3 lb. turkey parts	3 carrots, diced
1 onion	1/2 c. noodles
1 bunch celery leaves	Salt and pepper to taste

Combine the turkey parts, 1 1/2 quarts water, the onion and celery leaves in a large kettle and bring to a boil. Simmer for about 2 hours, then lift out the turkey and discard skin, bones, gristle and solid fat. Strain the broth and add turkey meat, carrots, noodles and seasonings. Noodles may be cut or broken in 2-inch lengths, if desired. Bring the broth mixture to a boil and reduce the heat. Simmer for about 10 minutes, then pour immediately into pint jars. Place the lid on each jar after filling and tighten. Process at 10 pounds pressure for 1 hour. Soups containing meat will keep longer if processed in pints.

Mrs. Victor Carlson, Montgomery, Alabama

FISH CHOWDER

5 lb. cleaned fish	3/4 lb. salt pork, diced
2 tsp. salt	1 c. chopped onions
4 peppercorns	2 qt. diced pared potatoes
1/4 hot red pepper	

Bone the fish and cut the fillets in 1-inch pieces. Chill until ready to use. Cook the bones, head and tail in 3 quarts water to make a fish stock. Add the seasonings and cook over low heat until fish falls from bones. Strain and reserve the stock. Cook the salt pork until brown and drain off fat. Add the onions to the pork and cook until tender. Combine the stock, fish, onion mixture and potatoes. Bring to a boil and cook for 10 minutes. Pour immediately into hot jars, allowing 1 inch at the top. Adjust the caps and process for 1 hour and 40 minutes at 10 pounds pressure. About 12 pints.

Mrs. Carl Johnson, Natchez, Mississippi

FISH STOCK

2 lb. whitefish	1 bay leaf
2 peppercorns	1 tbsp. diced carrot
1 whole clove	1 tbsp. diced celery
1 sprig of parsley	1 tbsp. diced onion

Cut the whitefish into small pieces into a Dutch oven and add 1 1/4 quarts water and remaining ingredients. Bring to a boil, then reduce the heat and cover. Simmer for about 1 hour, then strain through several thicknesses of cheesecloth. Bring to a boil again and pour into a hot sterilized pint jar, allowing 1 inch at the top. Adjust caps and process at 10 pounds pressure. Fish stock may be used for soups, chowders, creamed mixtures and bisques.

Mrs. Curtis Watson, Toccoa, Georgia

MANHATTAN CLAM CHOWDER

2 doz. large clams, cleaned	2 c. tomatoes
1/4 lb. salt pork, diced	2 potatoes, diced
2 lge. onions, chopped	4 c. water
1 carrot, diced	Dash of thyme
1 c. chopped celery	Salt and pepper to taste
1 green pepper, diced	Flour

Steam the clams in a small amount of water until shells open. Reserve the liquor and mince the clams. Brown the salt pork and remove cracklings from fat. Brown the onions, carrot, celery and green pepper lightly in fat, then add the tomatoes, potatoes, water, seasonings, minced clams and liquor. Thicken slightly with flour mixed in cold water. Bring to a boil and pour into hot pint jars. Adjust the jar caps and process for 1 hour and 40 minutes at 10 pounds pressure.

Mrs. G. N. Rogers, Richmond, Virginia

CRAB SOUP

8 c. crab meat	4 c. cooked tomatoes
1 c. butter	1/4 c. rice
2 c. diced green pepper	1 1/2 tbsp. salt
2 c. chopped celery	1 tsp. white pepper
2 c. minced onion	

Inspect the crab meat thoroughly and discard bits of shell. Wash and drain. Melt 1/2 cup butter in a large kettle, then add the pepper, celery and onion and cook until soft. Add the tomatoes. Melt the remaining butter in another saucepan and simmer the crab meat for 3 minutes. Add the crab meat to the vegetables. Add 3 1/2 gallons water and bring almost to boiling point. Add the rice, salt and white pepper, stirring to mix well. Pour immediately into hot pint jars, then fit with lids. Process for 1 hour and 40 minutes at 10 pounds pressure.

Mrs. Wilma Cook, Gulfport, Mississippi

BISQUE OF OYSTER

1/4 c. butter	1 qt. oysters
1/4 c. flour	1/2 c. chopped onion
1 tbsp. salt	1/4 c. diced celery
1/2 tsp. pepper	1 sprig of parsley
5 c. fish stock	1 bay leaf

Melt the butter in a saucepan and stir in the flour, salt and pepper. Add 2 cups fish stock gradually and cook, stirring constantly until slightly thickened. Chop the oysters and place in a saucepan with oyster liquor, 2 cups water and remaining ingredients. Simmer for about 30 minutes, then rub through a fine sieve and combine with the white sauce and remaining fish stock. Bring to a boil, then pour into hot sterilized pint jars. Adjust caps and process at 10 pounds pressure for 30 minutes. Milk or cream may be added, then heat and serve.

Mrs. Iris Hambley, Panama City, Florida

SEAFOOD CHOWDER

1 lb. scallops	1 pt. canned tomatoes
1 lb. shrimp	1 clove of garlic
1 lb. haddock	1/4 c. catsup
12 slices bacon, chopped	1/4 tsp. curry powder
1 c. chopped onion	2 tsp. salt
1 c. chopped celery	1/4 tsp. hot sauce
1/2 lemon, thinly sliced	1 tbsp. Worcestershire sauce

Clean and drain the scallops, shrimp and haddock and cut the haddock into 1-inch pieces. Cook the bacon until brown and add the onion and celery. Cook, covered, for 5 minutes, then drain. Add the lemon, 1 quart water, tomatoes, garlic, catsup, curry powder, salt and sauces and simmer for 10 minutes. Remove the garlic, if desired. Add the scallops, shrimp and haddock and bring to a boil. Pack immediately into hot jars and adjust the caps. Process for 1 hour and 30 minutes at 10 pounds pressure. Sherry to taste and a small amount of butter may be added, then heat and serve.

Mrs. F. L. Carter, Baltimore, Maryland

SPLIT PEA SOUP

2 c. split peas	2 carrots, sliced
1 ham hock	1 c. chopped celery
1 onion, chopped	Salt to taste

Soak the peas in water to cover for 12 hours and drain. Place in a large pot with 3 quarts water and ham hock and simmer, covered, for 2 hours. Add the onion, carrots and celery and simmer, covered, for 1 hour. Remove the ham hock and cut the meat into small pieces. Press the vegetables through a sieve and add the meat and salt. Pour into hot pint jars to 1 inch from the top. Process at 10 pounds pressure for 50 minutes.

Mrs. Jane Bertrand, Conway, Arkansas

OLD FAITHFUL NAVY BEAN SOUP

2 c. dried navy beans	1 carrot, thinly sliced
4 oz. salt pork, diced	1 c. finely diced potato
1/2 c. chopped onion	Salt and pepper to taste

Inspect the beans, discarding any that are discolored. Wash in cold water and drain. Cover with water and allow to soak overnight. Add the pork, vegetables and seasonings and bring to a boil. Reduce the heat, then cover the pan and simmer for 2 hours. Remove the meat and cut in small pieces. Press the vegetables through a sieve. Add the meat and boiling water, if needed, to thin the soup. Pour into hot pint jars and place the lids and rings on the jars. Process at 10 pounds pressure for 50 minutes.

Mrs. E. E. Bradford, Stephenville, Texas

SPICY TOMATO SOUP

1/2 bushel tomatoes	1 garlic clove
7 onions	1/2 lb. butter
14 strips of celery	1/4 c. salt
14 strips of parsley	1/2 tsp. pepper
14 bay leaves	1 1/2 c. brown sugar
21 cloves	2 c. flour

Combine the first 7 ingredients in a large kettle and simmer until soft, then press through a sieve. Add the butter, salt, pepper and brown sugar and cook for 10 minutes. Mix flour with enough water to make a thin paste. Add to the tomato mixture and bring to a boil. Put into hot, sterilized jars and seal. Process pints for 20 minutes and quarts for 30 minutes at 10 pounds pressure.

Mrs. Otto Hawley, Hattiesburg, Mississippi

HEARTY VEGETABLE SOUP

1 qt. cut corn	6 c. thickly sliced carrots
2 qt. peeled, cored chopped tomatoes	2 c. 1-in. slices of celery
	2 c. sliced onions
1 qt. green lima beans	Salt
6 med. potatoes, pared and cubed	

Combine the vegetables in a large kettle and add 1 1/2 quarts water. Bring to a boil and boil for 5 minutes. Pour immediately into hot jars, leaving 1 inch at the top. Add 1 teaspoon salt to each quart jar and 1/2 teaspoon salt to each pint jar. Fit with jar lids and rings and tighten. Process pints for 55 minutes and quarts for 1 hour and 25 minutes at 10 pounds pressure. About 7 quarts.

Mrs. Michael Walters, Oklahoma City, Oklahoma

VEGETABLE SOUP MIX

1/2 bushel tomatoes, chopped
1/2 bushel carrots, chopped
2 heads cabbage, shredded
1 lge. bunch celery, chopped

8 ripe peppers, chopped
Parsley, chopped
Salt

Place the vegetables in a large kettle, adding water to barely cover and bring to a boil. Add parsley. Pack in hot jars, adding 1 teaspoon salt to each quart jar. Place a lid and ring on each jar and tighten. Process for 35 minutes at 10 pounds pressure. 32 quarts.

Mrs. Ted Ellsworth, Little Rock, Arkansas

CABBAGE AND BEET SOUP

2 heads cabbage, shredded
5 c. diced cooked beets
2 onions, diced

1 gal. soup stock
2 tsp. salt
1/2 tsp. pepper

Combine all the ingredients in a large kettle and bring to a boil. Pour immediately into hot sterilized jars and adjust the lids. Process at 10 pounds pressure for 30 minutes. To serve, place a slice of bread in each soup bowl. Bring the soup to a boil, then pour over the bread. Sprinkle with grated cheese. About 4 quarts.

Mrs. Catherine Blakeley, Baton Rouge, Louisiana

OLD-FASHIONED TOMATO SOUP

1/2 bushel tomatoes, chopped
6 onions, chopped
2 tbsp. celery seed
1 c. sugar

1/4 tsp. red pepper
2 tbsp. salt
1 c. butter
1 c. flour

Combine the tomatoes, onions and celery seed in a large kettle. Boil over low heat for 1 hour. Strain, then add sugar, pepper and salt. Melt the butter and stir in the flour until smooth. Add to the tomato mixture and cook for 20 minutes longer. Pour into sterilized jars and seal. Process at 5 pounds pressure for 5 minutes. 13 pints.

Lelia P. McPeak, Bland, Virginia

MINESTRONE

1/2 c. dried beans
1 lb. bacon, chopped
1 lb. ham, chopped
1 lb. Italian sausage, chopped
8 onions, chopped
8 tomatoes, chopped
2 c. rice

1 c. diced celery
4 qt. beef stock
1 head cabbage, shredded
2 c. cut green beans
2 c. chopped carrots
1 tbsp. salt
1 tsp. pepper

Soak the dried beans in water to cover for 2 to 3 hours, then drain. Fry the bacon, ham, sausage and onions together until slightly browned. Add the tomatoes, rice, soaked beans, celery and beef stock and simmer until the beans are tender, skimming off the fat frequently. Add the remaining ingredients and bring to a boil. Pour into hot jars and cap each jar after filling. Process pints at 10 pounds pressure for 1 hour and quarts for 1 hour and 15 minutes. Water may be added, if desired for a thinner consistency when served. Serve with grated Parmesan cheese.

Mrs. H. R. Branch, Hot Springs, Arkansas

ITALIAN SPAGHETTI SAUCE

3 onions, chopped	1 tbsp. chili powder
4 cloves of garlic, minced	2 tsp. oregano
1/2 c. olive oil	2 bay leaves
4 lb. ground beef	2 qt. chopped tomatoes
1 tbsp. salt	1 qt. tomato sauce

Cook the onions and garlic in the hot oil in a skillet until golden. Add the ground beef and seasonings and brown lightly. Ground beef may have to be cooked in portions to brown evenly. Transfer to a large kettle, if necessary and add the remaining ingredients. Cover and simmer for 20 minutes. Remove and discard the bay leaves. Pour immediately into hot sterilized jars and place the lids and rings on the jars. Process pints for 1 hour and quarts for 1 hour and 15 minutes at 10 pounds pressure.

Mrs. Anna Garcia, El Paso, Texas

BARBECUE SAUCE

24 lge. ripe tomatoes	1 c. (firmly packed) brown sugar
2 med. onions, quartered	1 c. vinegar
2 c. chopped celery	2 cloves of garlic, crushed
1 1/2 c. chopped sweet green peppers	1 tbsp. salt
2 hot red peppers	1 tbsp. dry mustard
1 tsp. peppercorns	1 tbsp. paprika
2 c. chopped onions	1 tsp. hot sauce
	1/8 tsp. cayenne pepper

Peel, core and chop the tomatoes then combine with quartered onions, celery and peppers. Cook for about 30 minutes or until soft. Press through a fine sieve or food mill. Cook for about 45 minutes or until the mixture is reduced to about one-half. Tie the peppercorns in a cheesecloth bag and add with remaining ingredients. Cook, stirring frequently, over low heat for about 1 hour and 30 minutes or until the mixture is the consistency of catsup. Pour into hot jars, leaving 1/4-inch head space. Adjust caps. Process for 20 minutes in a boiling water bath. Add 1 cup salad oil to 1 pint jar Barbecue Sauce and mix thoroughly before using. 4 to 5 pints.

Mrs. Laurie Whitney, Shreveport, Louisiana

SPANISH SAUCE

1 c. butter	1/2 tsp. pepper
1 c. chopped onion	2 qt. strained tomato juice
1 c. flour	1 1/2 c. cooked chopped ham
1 1/2 tbsp. salt	1 1/2 c. chopped celery
1/2 tsp. cayenne	1 c. chopped carrots

Melt 1/2 cup butter, then add the onion and saute until lightly browned. Melt remaining butter and add to onion mixture. Blend in the flour, salt, cayenne and pepper. Add the tomato juice gradually, stirring constantly. Add the ham, celery and carrots and bring to a boil. Pack immediately into hot sterilized jars, leaving 1 inch at the top. Process at 10 pounds pressure for 50 minutes. May be served over rice or spaghetti.

Mrs. Jean Tuttle, Carlsbad, New Mexico

APPLE CHILI SAUCE

12 tomatoes, ground	2 c. vinegar
12 apples, ground	5 tsp. salt
8 onions, ground	4 c. sugar
12 sm. red peppers, ground	

Combine all the ingredients in a large kettle and simmer for 45 minutes or until the mixture thickens. Pour into hot, sterilized jars and seal. 6 pints.

Mrs. Ellen Morgan Schenck, Louisville, Kentucky

BASIC CHILI SAUCE

4 qt. peeled chopped tomatoes	2 tsp. cinnamon
1 1/2 c. chopped onions	1 tsp. cloves
2 c. chopped green peppers	1/2 tsp. nutmeg
1/4 c. salt	1 c. vinegar
1 c. sugar	

Combine all the ingredients and boil for about 1 hour or until thickened, stirring frequently. Pour into sterilized jars and seal immediately.

Mrs. Wyrtis W. Shadley, Vicksburg, Mississippi

CUCUMBER CHILI SAUCE

2 qt. ground cucumbers	1 1/2 tsp. white pepper
3 tbsp. salt	1/2 tsp. cinnamon
1 c. grated onion	1/2 tsp. dry mustard
2 1/2 c. vinegar	1/2 c. brown sugar

Mix the cucumbers and salt thoroughly and set aside for at least 30 minutes. Drain and squeeze to remove as much liquid as possible. Combine the cucumbers and onion. Combine the vinegar, spices and sugar in a saucepan and bring to a boil. Simmer for 5 minutes. Add the cucumber mixture and simmer for 5 minutes longer. Pour into hot sterilized jars and seal.

Mrs. Grace Coburn, Newport, Kentucky

GREEN CHILI SAUCE

6 lb. green tomatoes	2 1/2 c. cider vinegar
6 med. onions, peeled	1 tbsp. whole cloves
4 sweet green peppers	1 tbsp. whole allspice
1 1/2 c. sugar	2 sticks cinnamon, broken
2 1/2 tbsp. salt	

Core the tomatoes, then chop the tomatoes, onions and green peppers finely. Place in a large kettle and add the sugar, salt and vinegar. Tie the spices in a bag for easy removal, then add to the tomato mixture. Bring to a boil and reduce the heat. Simmer for about 3 hours or until the sauce is thick. Discard the spices and pour immediately into hot sterilized jars, then seal.

Mrs. Sara Jackson, Houston, Texas

TO MAKE AND CAN CHILI SAUCE

7 lb. (about) tomatoes	1 1/2 tbsp. light mustard seed
Red sweet peppers	1 long stick cinnamon
Bermuda onions	1 tsp. whole allspice
1 1/4 c. sugar	3/4 tsp. dried basil
2 tbsp. salt	1 bay leaf
1 lge. clove of garlic	2 1/2 c. 5 per cent acid
1 sm. pod hot red pepper	strength vinegar

Wash and drain the vegetables. Scald, core and skin the tomatoes. Discard the seed and heavy white ribs of the peppers. Skin the onions. Put the tomatoes through the coarse blade of a food chopper and measure. Four quarts should be the volume for chili sauce. Chop the sweet peppers and measure 2 cups. Chop the onions and measure 1 1/2 cups. Combine the tomatoes, peppers, onions, sugar and salt in a large kettle and cook until the juice runs freely. Increase the heat and boil, stirring frequently, for 30 to 40 minutes or until the mixture is reduced to about 1/2 of the original volume. Tie the garlic, hot pepper, spices and herbs in a thin, closely-woven cloth and add to the tomato mixture. Boil, stirring frequently, until the sauce is quite thick. Add the vinegar and boil until of desired consistency. Discard the spice bag and pour the hot sauce to about 1/8 inch of the top of the jar. Place the lids on the jars and screw the bands tight. Process for 5 minutes in boiling water in a waterbath canner. Let jars stand for about 12 hours. Test the seal, then remove the band and store in a cool, dark, dry place.

Photograph for this recipe on page 81.

HOT CHILI SAUCE

12 lge. ripe tomatoes	1 tsp. cinnamon
4 sm. green peppers	1 tsp. cloves
2 lge. onions	1 tsp. dry mustard
1/2 c. brown sugar	Hot sauce to taste
1/2 c. sugar	Chili powder to taste
4 tsp. salt	2 1/2 c. vinegar

Peel the tomatoes, then chop with green peppers and onions. Place in a cooking pot and add remaining ingredients. Cook over low heat for 1 hour and 30 minutes or until thick. Pour in sterilized jars and seal. Mix with 1 pound ground beef and 2 cans kidney beans, then heat and serve.

Mrs. Lynwood Vaughan, Luray, Virginia

RHUBARB SAUCE

2 qt. chopped rhubarb	1/2 c. vinegar
1/2 c. chopped onion	1 tsp. salt
1 1/2 c. chopped, seedless	1 tsp. cinnamon
raisins	1 tsp. ginger
3 1/2 c. (firmly packed)	1 tsp. allspice
brown sugar	

Combine the rhubarb, onion, raisins, sugar and vinegar. Cook for about 25 minutes or until thick. Stir frequently to prevent sticking. Add the salt and spices and cook for 5 minutes longer. Pour boiling sauce into sterilized jars, leaving 1/8-inch head space. Adjust caps and tighten to seal. About 4 pints.

Mrs. Ed York, Lexington, Kentucky

CRANBERRY CATSUP

2 1/2 lb. cranberries	1 tbsp. cinnamon
Vinegar	1 tsp. ground cloves
2 1/2 c. sugar	

Wash the cranberries thoroughly and drain. Place in a large pan and barely cover with vinegar. Bring to a boil, then reduce the heat. Simmer until the cranberries are soft, then press through a fine sieve. Add the sugar and spices and simmer until of desired consistency. Pour into hot sterilized jars and seal.

Mrs. Paula Longstreet, Knoxville, Tennessee

CRANBERRY SAUCE

1 lb. cranberries	2 c. sugar
2 c. port	

Place cranberries and port in a saucepan and bring to a boil. Cook for 6 minutes, then add the sugar but do not stir. Boil briskly for 10 minutes longer, then reduce heat as low as possible and allow the mixture to simmer for 10 minutes. Pour into half-pint jars and seal.

Mrs. Harold Davidson, Houston, Texas

HOT PEPPER SAUCE

24 (about) long hot peppers	2 tbsp. mixed pickling spices
10 lge. ripe tomatoes	1 c. sugar
4 qt. vinegar	1 tbsp. salt

Wash the vegetables thoroughly and drain. Remove the seeds, then chop the peppers. Core and chop the tomatoes. Combine the vegetables and 2 cups vinegar in a large kettle and bring to a boil. Boil until soft, then press through a fine sieve. Tie the spices in a bag and add with the sugar and salt to the pepper mixture. Boil until the sauce is thick, then add the remaining vinegar and boil for about 15 minutes longer. Discard the spices and pour the boiling sauce into hot sterilized jars.

Mrs. Hallie Williston, Farmington, New Mexico

SPICY TOMATO CATSUP

1 gal. ripe tomatoes	1 tbsp. dry mustard
1 c. vinegar	1/2 tbsp. cloves
1 tbsp. salt	1 tsp. pepper
1 1/2 tbsp. allspice	1/4 tsp. red pepper

Wash the tomatoes thoroughly and drain, then core and chop. Cover over low heat until soft, then strain through a sieve. Combine the puree and remaining ingredients in a large kettle and bring to a boil. Simmer, stirring frequently, for about 4 hours. Pour into hot sterilized jars and seal immediately.

Mrs. Cliff Ellis, Brunswick, Georgia

TOMATO CATSUP

1 c. coarse salt	6 hot peppers
1 gal. ripe tomatoes, chopped fine	1 qt. vinegar
1 gal. cabbage, chopped fine	6 c. sugar
1 qt. onions, chopped	1 tbsp. pickling spice, tied in a bag

Combine the salt, tomatoes and cabbage and pour into a cloth bag. Hang and allow to drain overnight. Place the drained mixture and remaining ingredients in a large pan and boil for 30 minutes. Remove the spice bag and pour catsup into sterilized jars. Seal.

Mrs. C. L. McKinney, Crofton, Kentucky

TOMATO-CELERY SAUCE

7 lb. ripe tomatoes, peeled	4 c. cider vinegar
2 bunches celery	3 c. sugar
2 sweet green peppers, seeded	4 tsp. salt
10 onions, peeled	6 sm. hot red peppers

Chop the tomatoes, celery, peppers and onions with the medium blade of a food chopper. Combine all the ingredients in a large kettle and bring to a boil. Simmer, stirring occasionally, for about 2 hours or until thick. Discard the hot peppers and pour into hot sterilized jars.

Mrs. Herman Starr, Owensboro, Kentucky

PIZZA SAUCE

6 lb. ground beef	5 lge. sweet pickles, diced
2 lb. sausage	3 tsp. oregano
7 c. tomato paste	3 tbsp. salt
2 onions, diced	2 tsp. pepper

Combine the ground beef and sausage in a skillet and cook over medium heat, stirring constantly, until brown. Drain off fat. Add remaining ingredients, then cover and simmer for about 30 minutes, stirring frequently. Pack into hot sterilized jars, leaving room for expansion. Place lids and rings on the jars and tighten. Process at 10 pounds pressure for 1 hour and 15 minutes. Use one quart sauce per pizza. Top with pepperoni or mushrooms and grated cheese. 7 quarts.

Mrs. Edna Riley, El Paso, Texas

GRAPE CATSUP

5 lb. Concord grapes	1 tbsp. whole cloves
2 c. cider vinegar	1 tbsp. whole allspice
6 1/2 c. sugar	2 pieces whole mace
1 1/2 tsp. salt	2 gingerroots
1 stick cinnamon, broken	

Wash and stem the grapes, then place in a large preserving kettle and simmer until tender, stirring frequently. Press the grapes through a sieve. Add the vinegar, sugar and salt to the grape pulp. Tie the spices in a bag and add to the grape mixture. Bring to a boil and reduce the heat. Simmer, stirring frequently, for about 35 minutes or until of desired consistency. Discard the spices and pour into hot sterilized jars and seal.

Mrs. Olin Green, Athens, Georgia

MEXICAN SAUCE

1 qt. tomato sauce	2 tbsp. chopped onion
1 tsp. sugar	1 tbsp. lemon juice

| 1/2 c. 1-in. pieces of
celery
1/8 tsp. basil | 2 tbsp. chopped red or green
sweet pepper
8 drops of hot sauce |

Combine all the ingredients in a large kettle and cook over moderate heat until the celery is tender-crisp. Fill hot sterilized jars to 1/2 inch of the top. Wipe the tops clean. Place the lids on jars and screw the bands tight. Process for 45 minutes in boiling water in a waterbath canner.

PLAIN TOMATO SAUCE

| **Firm ripe tomatoes** | **Salt** |

Wash, rinse, drain and core the fresh firm tomatoes. Cut in 2-inch pieces and place in a large kettle. Cover and cook over low heat until the juice runs freely. Remove the cover and cook over high heat, stirring frequently, until the tomatoes are mushy. Put the tomatoes through a food mill or sieve to remove the skins and seed. Return the pulp to the kettle and cook until almost as thick as catsup. Pour the hot sauce to 1/4 inch from the top of the jars and add 1 teaspoon salt to each jar. Place the lids on the jars and screw the bands tight. Process pints and quarts in boiling water in a waterbath canner for 30 minutes.

Plain Tomato Sauce (above); Mexican Sauce (page 80); Chili Sauce (page 77)

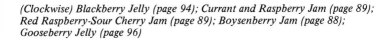

(Clockwise) Blackberry Jelly (page 94); Currant and Raspberry Jam (page 89); Red Raspberry-Sour Cherry Jam (page 89); Boysenberry Jam (page 88); Gooseberry Jelly (page 96)

jams, jellies, and marmalades

Years ago, the pride of a southern homemaker was the shelves where her jams, jellies, and marmalades gleamed in their jars like jewels. Very special friends or visitors would be honored by the presentation of one of these jars; if the homemaker felt particularly warm toward her friend, the recipe might be given along with the jar.

This custom is recalled by the section that follows, full of page after page of home-tested, family-prized recipes for jams, jellies, and marmalades. Prefacing these recipes are two pages of the latest time-saving and proven methods for preparing these tasty foods. Together, the recipes and information will bring you hours of cooking pleasure.

Look, for example, at the recipe for Jam of 4 Berries. By combining strawberries, raspberries, currants, and cherries, you get a subtle flavor combination and a rich red color that adds to the delight of tasting this jam. Then, there's an unusual recipe for Bell Pepper Jelly, the perfect accompaniment to meat, poultry, or seafood. It combines bell peppers and hot red peppers in a jelly that will add sparkle to any dinner. Orange-Lemon Jelly takes two popular citrus fruits and blends them into a crystal clear, attractive yellow-orange jelly that is delightful on toast or as a filling for cookies or tarts.

These are just some of the recipes awaiting you in the pages that follow. Browse through this section now, and enjoy these recipes for jams, jellies, and marmalades.

The fun foods in canning, and often the ones that provide the most satisfaction for the home canner, are jellies, jams, and marmalades. Jellies are clear semisolid preserves that are firm enough to hold their shape when unmolded from the jar, yet soft enough to spread with a knife. Jams are smooth fruit spreads that are less firm than jellies; they contain evenly distributed pieces of fruit that make them thicker than jellies. Marmalades are sweet preserves that usually contain shredded, chopped, sliced, or ground fruit rind. They should be clearer and firmer than jams.

The substance that causes all these foods to become relatively firm is *pectin*, a natural thickening agent present in all fruits. Underripe fruit usually contains sufficient natural pectin to cause gelling, although many recipes specify the use of liquid or powdered commercial pectin to assure a flawless product.

Although there is a marked difference in the consistencies and textures of

instructions

FOR JAMS, JELLIES AND MARMALADES

jams, jellies, and marmalades, there are several preliminary preparations common to each. Review the section on "Successful Canning and Preserving" on pages 9 and 10 and carefully read the following general instructions before beginning any preparations.

1. Read your recipe carefully. Follow the manufacturer's instructions for filling and sealing canning jars and jelly glasses. Assemble all the equipment and ingredients that you will need.

2. Check your jars and glasses for nicks, cracks, or rough edges. Wash them in hot soapy water and rinse thoroughly. Scald the jars or glasses in boiling water for 10 to 15 minutes. Drain and invert them on a towel or rubber tray. Rinse caps for jelly glasses and scald self-sealing caps.

3. If your recipe specifies liquid or powdered pectin, use fully ripened fruit. For recipes requiring no additional pectin, use a combination of 3/4 ripe and 1/4 underripe fruit to assure the proper amount of natural pectin necessary to jell the mixture. Imperfect or irregularly shaped fruit may be used as long as spoiled and bruised portions are carefully removed and discarded.

4. Wash the fruit gently in cold running water or in several changes of water. Lift the fruit out of the water. Sort. Remove the hulls, stems, skins, pits, or seeds; leave whole, slice, chop, or crush according to the recipe instructions.

5. Use a large heavy kettle of 8 to 10 quart capacity, with a broad flat bottom. This size kettle will allow the jam, jelly, or marmalade to bubble and cook rapidly within the confines of the kettle.

6. Prepare the fruit as directed in the recipe. Cook only small batches at a time; do not double recipes.

For jellies . . .

1. Extract the fruit juice according to recipe directions. Wet a jelly bag or several layers of cheesecloth and wring the water from it. Place juice in cloth and let the juice drip through without squeezing or pressing the jelly bag. Or, to obtain the maximum yield of juice, squeeze or press the bag until most of the juice is extracted. If the latter method is used, re-strain the juice through a clean damp jelly bag without squeezing.
2. Pour the fruit juice into the kettle and begin cooking. For jelly without added pectin, stir the sugar into the juice until it dissolves. For jelly with added pectin, follow the pectin manufacturer's instructions.
3. Boil the mixture rapidly to the jellying point. To test jelly, dip a large metal spoon into the boiling syrup. Tilt the spoon so that the syrup runs over the side. When the drops of syrup merge and break from the spoon in a sheet, leaving the spoon clean, the jellying point is reached. On a candy thermometer this "sheeting stage" usually registers 9 degrees above the boiling point of water in your locality.
4. Remove the jelly from the heat and quickly skim the foam.
5. Fill and seal one jar at a time with the boiling hot jelly. Leave 1/8 inch head space in standard canning jars, 1/4 inch in jelly glasses. Wipe the top and thread of each jar with a clean damp cloth. Adjust the lid on the canning jar according to the manufacturer's instructions. Invert the jar for 30 seconds so that the hot jelly can destroy mold or yeast that may have settled on the jelly. Stand the jar upright. Remove the lid and cover jelly immediately with hot paraffin.
6. Allow the jars to stand, undisturbed, overnight or until cool. Cover jelly glasses with metal lids. Remove bands from lids of canning jars. (If the product was not hot enough to produce a seal, the bands must be left on to keep the jars tightly closed.)
7. Store jelly in a dark, dry, cool area.

For jams and marmalades . . .

1. Place the fruit in the kettle and begin cooking over low heat. For jams and marmalades without added pectin, add the sugar to the fruit, stirring to dissolve completely. For jams and marmalades with added pectin, follow the pectin manufacturer's instructions.
2. After the sugar has dissolved, bring the mixture to a boil and cook until the jellying point is reached. (See previous step 3 above.) Stir the mixture frequently as it thickens to prevent sticking and scorching.
3. Remove the fruit mixture from the heat. Fill and seal canning jars or jelly glasses one at a time as directed in previous steps 5 and 6 above.
4. If you live in an exceptionally warm area or if your storage area is not sufficiently cool and dry, process hot jams and marmalades 10 minutes in a boiling water-bath canner at 212 degrees after sealing.
5. Cool and store jams and marmalades as you would jellies.

APRICOT JAM

2 qt. crushed peeled apricots	6 c. sugar 1/4 c. lemon juice

Combine the apricots, sugar and lemon juice in a large kettle and bring to a boil over low heat, stirring until the sugar dissolves. Cook over medium heat, stirring frequently, for about 25 minutes. Jam is thick enough when mixture will sheet from a spoon. Pour boiling jam into hot sterilized jars and seal. About 5 pints.

Mrs. Gale Crawford, Sarasota, Florida

BLACKBERRY JAM

6 c. blackberries 6 c. sugar 1 c. orange juice	1/4 c. lemon juice 1 tbsp. grated orange rind

Combine the blackberries and 1/2 cup water in a large kettle and cook until soft. Press the blackberries through a sieve or a food mill, then add the sugar, fruit juices and grated rind. Cook over high heat, stirring to prevent sticking, until the liquid sheets from a spoon. Pour, boiling hot, into sterilized jars and seal.

Mrs. Dolores Pihi, Orlando, Florida

FIG JAM

5 lb. (about) fresh figs 6 c. sugar	1/4 c. lemon juice

Pour boiling water over the figs and let stand for 10 minutes, then drain. Stem and chop the figs, then measure. Five pounds should yield about 2 quarts. Add 3/4 cup water and the sugar to the figs and bring to a boil, stirring to dissolve the sugar. Cook and stir over medium heat until thick. Add the lemon juice and cook for 1 minute longer. Pour immediately into hot sterilized jars and seal. About 5 pints.

Mrs. Dee Grant, Columbus, Mississippi

JAM OF FOUR BERRIES

1 qt. strawberries 1 qt. raspberries 1 qt. red currants	1 qt. morello cherries 6 1/2 c. sugar

Rinse the strawberries carefully and drain, then remove the stems. Examine the raspberries, but do not rinse. Rinse the currants and remove the stems. Rinse the cherries and remove the stones. Place the cherries in a large saucepan and cook over low heat for about 10 minutes. Add the strawberries, currants and raspberries and bring to a simmer. Simmer for 5 minutes. Shake the pan occasionally, but do not stir with a spoon. Add the sugar and simmer for about 30 minutes or until the syrup is thick. Pour the jam into hot sterilized jars and seal.

Photograph for this recipe on cover.

GOOSEBERRY JAM

1 lb. gooseberries   1 lb. sugar

Wash the gooseberries thoroughly and drain. Remove the stems and crush slightly. Cook over low heat until the gooseberries are soft, then add the sugar, stirring until dissolved. Cook until the juice sheets from a spoon as for jelly. Pour into hot sterilized glasses and seal. Use 3/4 pound sugar per pound gooseberries if ripe ones are used. About two 6-ounce glasses.

Mrs. Eula West, Covington, Kentucky

MATRIMONY JAM

3 c. chopped peeled, pitted   3 c. chopped pared, cored
  ripe plums   cooking apples
3 c. chopped pared, cored   1 c. cut-up orange sections
  firm pears   6 c. sugar

Combine the plums, pears, apples, orange sections and 1/2 cup water in a large kettle. Bring to a boil, then reduce the heat and simmer, covered, for 20 minutes. Add the sugar and stir over moderate heat until dissolved. Boil over high heat, stirring frequently, for 25 to 40 minutes or until moderately thickened. Do not overcook. Remove from heat and ladle immediately into hot jelly jars or canning jars. Fill to within 1/8 inch of tops and screw caps on evenly and tightly. Invert for several seconds and stand jars upright to cool. Seven 8-ounce jars or 3 to 4 pints.

Matrimony Jam (above), Parsley Jelly (page 96)

BOYSENBERRY JAM

2 qt. ripe boysenberries	1 box powdered fruit pectin
7 c. sugar	

Crush the boysenberries, one layer at a time. Press half the pulp through a sieve to remove some of the seed, if desired. Measure 5 cups boysenberries into a large saucepan. Measure the sugar and set aside. Mix the fruit pectin into the boysenberries. Place over high heat and stir until the boysenberry mixture comes to a rolling boil. Add the sugar all at once, stirring constantly. Bring to a boil and boil for 1 minute, stirring constantly. Remove from heat and skim off foam with a metal spoon. Stir and skim for 5 minutes to prevent the boysenberries from floating to the surface. Ladle into sterilized jelly glasses. Cover at once with 1/8 inch hot paraffin. 8 3/4 cups or about eleven 6-ounce glasses.

Photograph for this recipe on page 82.

SPICED GRAPE JAM

5 lb. grapes	1 c. vinegar
5 c. sugar	6 tbsp. whole cloves
4 to 6 tbsp. ground cinnamon	

Wash the grapes and drain. Remove pulp and reserve hulls. Place the pulp in a saucepan and cook over low heat until soft. Press through a colander to remove seeds. Add 1 cup water to each cup reserved hulls and place in a kettle. Cook over low heat until tender. Add the pulp, sugar, cinnamon and vinegar. Tie the cloves in a cheesecloth bag and add to grape mixture. Mix well. Cook over low heat for 1 hour or until thick, stirring frequently. Remove cheesecloth bag. Pour into sterilized pint jars and seal. Process in hot water bath for 15 minutes. 5-6 pints.

Mrs. Ben Elkin, Beulaville, North Carolina

MANGO JAM

30 sm. yellow mangoes	10 c. sugar
1 c. lemon juice	

Wash and peel the mangoes. Add water to within 1 inch of the top of the mangoes. Boil for 30 minutes and cool. Squeeze each pit until dry and press the pulp through a fine sieve. Measure the pulp. Thirty mangoes should produce about 10 cups. Add the lemon juice and sugar and boil until thick and clear. Pour into hot sterilized jars or glasses and seal.

Mrs. Norma Root, Palm Beach, Florida

BLUEBERRY-CURRANT JAM

1 qt. stemmed blueberries	3 c. sugar
2 c. stemmed currants	

Combine the blueberries and 1 cup water in a saucepan and cook over low heat for 5 minutes. Combine the currants and 1 cup water in another saucepan and cook for 10 minutes. Press through a sieve or food mill. Combine the pulp from the blueberries and the currants and cook over high heat for 5 minutes. Add the sugar, stirring until the sugar dissolves. Cook, stirring frequently, over high heat for about 20 minutes. Pour immediately into hot pint jars and seal. 2 pints.

Mrs. Pat Caney, Dundalk, Maryland

CURRANT AND RASPBERRY JAM

1 qt. ripe red currants
1 qt. red raspberries

7 c. sugar
1/2 bottle liquid fruit pectin

Remove the stems from the currants, then crush thoroughly. Press half the raspberries through a sieve to remove some of the seeds, if desired. Crush the remaining raspberries thoroughly. Combine the fruits to measure 4 1/2 cups and place in a large saucepan. Add the sugar to the fruits and mix thoroughly. Bring to a boil over high heat and boil rapidly for 1 minute, stirring constantly. Remove from the heat and stir in the fruit pectin immediately. Skim off the foam with a metal spoon. Stir and skim for 5 minutes to prevent the fruit from floating. Ladle into hot sterilized glasses and cover with 1/8 inch hot paraffin. 8 3/4 cups or about eleven 6-ounce glasses.

Photograph for this recipe on page 82.

RED RASPBERRY-SOUR CHERRY JAM

1 1/2 pt. ripe red
  raspberries
1 pt. ripe sour cherries

5 1/4 c. sugar
1 box powdered fruit pectin

Crush the raspberries, then measure 1 1/2 cups into a large pan. Pit and grind the sour cherries then measure 1 1/2 cups into the pan with the raspberries. Combine the sugar and fruits and mix thoroughly. Let stand for 10 minutes. Mix 3/4 cup water and the fruit pectin in a small saucepan. Bring to a boil and boil for 1 minute, stirring constantly. Add the boiling pectin mixture to the fruits and stir for about 2 minutes. Ladle quickly into jelly glasses or jars. Cover immediately with tight lids. Let stand at room temperature until set, then store in the freezer.

Photograph for this recipe on page 82.

FRENCH JAM

1 pt. finely chopped rhubarb
1 pt. finely chopped fresh
  pineapple

1 c. fresh strawberries
2 lb. sugar
1 tbsp. grated lemon rind

Combine the rhubarb, pineapple, strawberries and sugar in a shallow saucepan and let stand for 1 hour. Cover and cook slowly for 20 minutes, stirring occasionally. Add the lemon rind and boil, uncovered, until clear and thick. Pour in sterilized jars and seal. 8 glasses.

Mrs. Adrianna H. Mills, Johnson, Arkansas

89

Strawberry Melba Jam (below)

STRAWBERRY MELBA JAM

6 c. pureed strawberries	3 tbsp. orange liqueur
3 c. raspberries	1 tsp. grated lemon rind
6 c. sugar	2 tbsp. lemon juice

Combine all the ingredients in a large kettle. Bring to a boil over low heat, stirring almost constantly. Cook over moderate heat, stirring frequently, for 30 to 45 minutes or until slightly thickened. Do not overcook. Remove from heat and ladle immediately into hot jelly jars or canning jars. Fill to within 1/8 inch of tops and screw caps on evenly and tightly. Invert for several seconds and stand jars upright to cool. Seven 8-ounce jars or 3 to 4 pints.

JEWEL JAM

1 pt. pitted red cherries	7 c. sugar
10 oz. sliced strawberries	1/2 c. lemon juice
20 oz. sliced peaches	1 bottle liquid pectin

Canned cherries and thawed frozen strawberries and peaches may be used for this attractive jam. Chop the fruits in a blender, then combine with sugar, and lemon juice in a large kettle. Bring to a boil and boil, stirring constantly, for 1 minute. Remove from heat and stir in the pectin. Stir, skimming the foam from the top, for 5 minutes. Pour into hot, sterilized glasses, leaving 1/4 inch at the top. Cover with about 1/8 inch hot paraffin.

Mrs. Fred Clifford, Estelline, Texas

HOLIDAY CRANBERRY JAM

2 c. fresh cranberries	1 10-oz. package frozen
1 med. orange	strawberries, thawed and
1/2 c. water	crushed
3 c. sugar	1/4 bottle liquid fruit pectin

Finely chop or grind the cranberries. Cut the orange in quarters and remove the seeds, then grind. Combine the chopped fruits, water, sugar and crushed strawberries in a large kettle. Cook over low heat for 2 minutes, stirring constantly, then bring to a rolling boil. Boil hard for 1 minute, stirring constantly. Remove from heat and stir in the pectin and skim off foam. Stir for 4 to 5 minutes, then pour into sterilized jars and cover with 1/8 inch paraffin.

Mrs. Eleanor Brunski, Birmingham, Alabama

WINTER JAM

3 c. fresh cranberries	Juice and grated rind of 1 lemon
1 c. diced peeled apples	1 c. canned crushed pineapple
1 1/2 c. water	3 c. sugar

Place the cranberries and apples in a saucepan and cover with water. Cook until tender, then press fruits with juices through a strainer to remove skins. Add the lemon juice and rind, pineapple and sugar. Mix thoroughly in a deep kettle. Bring to a boil over high heat and boil, stirring constantly until jam becomes thick and clear. Pour in hot jars and seal. Four 8-ounce jars.

Mrs. Mamie Rice, Kershaw, South Carolina

PEACH JAM

4 c. chopped ripe peaches	1/2 bottle liquid fruit
1/4 c. lemon juice	pectin
7 1/2 c. sugar	

Combine the peaches and lemon juice in a large saucepan, then add the sugar, stirring to dissolve. Place over high heat and bring to a full rolling boil. Boil for 1 minute, stirring constantly. Remove from heat and stir in the pectin at once. Skim off foam with a metal spoon. Stir and skim by turns for 5 minutes to cool slightly and to prevent fruit from floating. Ladle quickly into glasses. Cover jam at once with 1/8 inch hot paraffin. About 11 medium glasses.

Photograph for this recipe on page 26.

PEAR AND APPLE JAM

1 pt. diced pears	Juice and grated rind of 1 lemon
1 pt. diced apples	3 1/2 c. sugar

Combine the pears, apples, lemon juice and rind and sugar in a large kettle. Cook, stirring until the sugar is dissolved, over high heat until the pear mixture is thick and clear. Pour into hot sterilized jars and seal.

Mrs. Betty Avinger, Columbia, South Carolina

MUSCADINE JAM

4 qt. muscadines	12 c. sugar

Wash the muscadines thoroughly and drain. Remove the pulp from the hulls. Chop the hulls, if desired, then cook for 15 to 20 minutes, adding a small amount of water to prevent sticking. Cook the pulp until soft and press through a sieve. Combine the pulp, hulls and sugar. Stir to dissolve sugar and bring to a boil over low heat. Cook for about 10 minutes, watching carefully to prevent the jam from becoming too thick. Pour into hot sterilized jars and seal. About 6 pints.

Mrs. Hannah Alford, Atlanta, Georgia

SPICED PEACH JAM

4 c. chopped ripe peaches	1/2 tsp. cloves
1/2 c. lemon juice	1/2 tsp. allspice
7 1/2 c. sugar	1/2 6-oz. bottle liquid
1 tsp. cinnamon	fruit pectin

Combine the peaches and lemon juice, then add the sugar and spices and mix well. Place over high heat and bring to a full rolling boil. Boil for 1 minute, stirring constantly. Remove from heat and stir in pectin immediately. Skim off foam and cool slightly. Stir, skimming off foam, for 5 minutes. Ladle into hot sterilized jars and seal. 3 pints.

Gertrude Jones, Byhalia, Mississippi

PINEAPPLE JAM

1 lge. fresh pineapple	1/2 lemon, thinly sliced
2 1/2 c. sugar	

Pare and core the pineapple, then chop fine. Combine the pineapple, sugar, 1 cup water and the lemon slices in a Dutch oven and place over low heat. Bring to a boil, stirring until the sugar dissolves. Boil over high heat, stirring frequently for about 30 minutes or until the jam sheets from a spoon. Pour immediately into hot sterilized jars and seal. About 3 half-pints.

Mrs. Isabelle Stoner, Carlsbad, New Mexico

RED PLUM JAM

3 1/2 c. sugar   4 c. coarsely ground plums

Pour the sugar over the plums and let stand for 1 hour. Cook over medium heat, stirring frequently, until the jam sheets from a spoon. Pour into hot sterilized jars and seal. 3 pints.

Mrs. Jeanette H. Bales, Chattanooga, Tennessee

GOLDEN RHUBARB JAM

5 c. diced rhubarb   1 lb. orange section candy,
5 c. sugar   chopped

Combine all the ingredients and let stand until the sugar is almost dissolved. Bring to a boil, stirring constantly, then cook and stir for 10 minutes or until mixture thickens. Place in sterilized jelly glasses or pint jars and seal. 4 pints.

Edythe B. Swalstad, Morganfield, Kentucky

MOCK STRAWBERRY JAM

6 c. mashed fresh figs   2 pkg. strawberry gelatin
3 c. sugar

Cut the stems from the figs, then wash thoroughly and drain. Crush to pulp, using a potato masher. Place all the ingredients in a large pot and cook over medium heat until the mixture starts to bubble. Reduce heat and cook for 45 minutes longer, stirring frequently.4-5 pints.

Mrs. Irvin Derangeo, Sunset, Louisiana

STRAWBERRY JAM

3 c. large firm strawberries   3 c. sugar

Wash the strawberries carefully and remove the caps and stems. Crush the strawberries and add the sugar. Cook over medium heat until the mixture sheets from a spoon. Pour into hot sterilized jars or jelly glasses and seal.

Hazel Patterson, Decatur, Alabama

BELL PEPPER JELLY

3/4 c. ground bell pepper   1 1/2 c. apple cider vinegar
1/4 c. red hot pepper   1 bottle fruit pectin
6 1/2 c. sugar

Combine all the ingredients except pectin in a heavy saucepan and bring to a boil over high heat. Remove from heat and let stand for 5 minutes. Add the fruit pectin and pour immediately into jelly jars. Seal.

Velma Hudson, Hereford, Texas

Lovers of Lime Jelly (below)

LOVERS OF LIME JELLY

3 lge. green limes	3 c. sugar
1 lge. lemon	3 drops green food coloring
1 sm. underripe apple	1 drop yellow food coloring

Wash and dry the fruits carefully. Use a sharp knife to remove the thin yellow part of the lemon peel. Leave as much of the white part as possible. Put the limes, lemon and apple through a food chopper, then measure. Add 3 cups cool water for each cup chopped fruit. Cover and let stand for 12 to 24 hours. Bring to a boil over medium heat and boil for 20 minutes, then pour into a bowl. Cover and let stand for 12 to 24 hours. Turn into a jelly bag and let drip for several hours. Do not press or squeeze the jelly bag. The natural pale color of lime jelly may be retained, if desired, by omitting the food coloring. Measure 3 cups lime stock into a large kettle, then add the sugar and food coloring. Place over high heat and stir until the sugar dissolves. Boil over high heat until the jelly sheets from a spoon. Skim foam quickly and pour into jelly glasses and seal.

BLACKBERRY JELLY

2 qt. ripe blackberries	1 box powdered fruit pectin
6 c. sugar	

Crush the blackberries and place in a cloth or jelly bag. Squeeze out the juice and measure 3 cups juice into a large pan. Add the sugar to the juice, stirring to mix well. Mix 3/4 cup water and the fruit pectin in a small saucepan and bring to a boil. Boil for 1 minute, stirring frequently. Add to the sweetened blackberry juice and stir for about 3 minutes. Pour quickly into hot sterilized jars and cover immediately with tight lids. Let stand at room temperature until set. Store in the refrigerator if jelly will be used within 2 or 3 weeks. About eight 6-ounce jars.

Photograph for this recipe on page 82.

GRAPE JELLY

3 1/2 lb. ripe Concord grapes	**6 c. sugar**
1 box powdered pectin	**Paraffin**

Stem the grapes and crush thoroughly in a large kettle. Add 1 1/2 cups water and bring to a boil. Simmer, covered, for 10 minutes. Place in a jelly cloth and squeeze out juice. Measure out 5 cups juice into a large saucepan. Add the pectin to the juice and mix well. Place over high heat. Cook and stir until mixture comes to a boil, then stir in sugar all at once. Bring to a rolling boil and boil for 1 minute, stirring constantly. Remove from heat and skim off foam. Pour into sterilized glasses and cover with 1/8 inch hot paraffin.

Mrs. Eardene Horton, Camden, Arkansas

SPICED GRAPE JELLY

3 lb. Concord grapes	**7 c. sugar**
1/2 c. cider vinegar	**1/2 c. bottled fruit pectin**
2 tsp. ground cinnamon	**1/2 lb. paraffin, melted**
1 tsp. ground cloves	

Wash, drain and crush the grapes thoroughly. Blend the vinegar, cinnamon and cloves and mix thoroughly with the grapes. Bring to a boil, then reduce heat and cover. Simmer for 10 minutes. Remove the mixture from heat and strain through a jelly bag. Measure 4 cups strained juice and bring to simmering point. Add the sugar and stir until dissolved, then bring mixture rapidly to a boil and stir in fruit pectin immediately. Boil rapidly for 1 minute, stirring constantly. Remove from heat and skim off any foam. Fill glasses immediately and cover with paraffin. 8 half-pints.

Mrs. Donald Bitting, St. Petersburg, Florida

GRAPEFRUIT JELLY

2 grapefruit	**3 c. sugar**

Peel the grapefruit and cut in quarters. Remove the seed. Grind the grapefruit through a food chopper. Measure the pulp. Add 3 cups water to each cup pulp and mix. Let stand overnight. Simmer for 20 to 30 minutes or until the pulp is tender. Drain, reserving 3 cups hot liquid. Stir the sugar into reserved liquid until dissolved and cook rapidly to soft-ball stage. Cool slightly, then pour into sterilized jars. Seal tightly. Jelly may become stiff before bottling is finished. Reheat to pouring stage. Do not return to a boil.

Mrs. Daniel Howell, Meridian, Mississippi

PARSLEY JELLY

2 lge. bunches parsley	2 tsp. grated lime rind
3 qt. water	1/2 c. lime juice
5 c. sugar	1/2 bottle liquid fruit pectin

Wash the parsley well and place in a kettle with the water. Bring to a boil, then reduce heat and simmer, covered, for 20 minutes. Strain and discard the parsley. Measure the juice, then return to the kettle and boil rapidly until reduced to 3 cups. Combine 3 cups juice, sugar and lime rind in a 4-quart saucepan or kettle. Stir over moderate heat until the sugar dissolves and mixture comes to a boil. Stir in the liquid pectin all at once. Bring to a full rolling boil, stirring constantly, and boil hard for 1 minute. Remove from heat. Stir in a few drops of green food coloring if desired. Skim off foam quickly and ladle into hot jelly glasses or jelly jars. Fill the glasses to within 1/2 inch of top and the jars to within 1/8 inch of top. Seal the glasses with paraffin and the jars with lids. Five 8-ounce glasses or jars.

Photographs for this recipe on pages 87 and 97.

CORNCOB JELLY

12 red corncobs	4 c. sugar
1 box powdered fruit pectin	

Wash the corncobs thoroughly, then chop in small pieces. Place in a heavy saucepan and add 3 quarts water. Simmer for 20 minutes or until liquid boils down to measure 3 cups. Strain, then add the fruit pectin. Stir to dissolve thoroughly and add sugar. Bring to a boil and boil for 1 minute. Pour immediately into hot sterilized jars and seal.

Martha Sue Carter, Powersburg, Kentucky

CRANBERRY JELLY

1 qt. cranberries	2 c. sugar
1 1/4 c. water	

Boil the cranberries in water until skins burst, then press through a colander. Add the sugar to the juice and stir until dissolved. Pour into cups and set in a cold place until jelled. Jelly will not set if mixture is boiled after sugar is added.

Mrs. W. K. Lokey, Lubbock, Texas

GOOSEBERRY JELLY

3 lb. ripe gooseberries	1/2 bottle liquid fruit
7 c. sugar	pectin

Crush or grind the gooseberries, a small amount at a time. Add 1/2 cup water, then bring to a boil and simmer, covered, for 10 minutes. Place in a jelly cloth or bag and squeeze out the juice. Measure 4 cups juice into a large saucepan. Combine the sugar and juice in a saucepan and mix thoroughly. Place over high heat and bring to a boil, stirring constantly. Stir in fruit pectin, then bring to a full rolling boil and boil hard for 1 minute, stirring constantly. Remove from heat, then skim off the foam with a metal spoon and pour quickly into hot sterilized glasses. Cover at once with 1/8 inch hot paraffin. 8 cups or ten 6-ounce glasses.

Photograph for this recipe on page 82.

RHUBARB-STRAWBERRY JELLY

6 c. sliced unpeeled rhubarb	3 1/4 c. sugar
1 c. water	1 bottle liquid fruit pectin
1 pt. strawberries	

Place the sliced rhubarb and water in a saucepan and bring to a boil. Reduce heat and simmer, covered, for 10 to 15 minutes or until the rhubarb is soft and comes apart in strings. Wash and hull the strawberries, then mash or puree in a blender. Remove the rhubarb from heat and add the pureed strawberries. Place a colander or strainer over a bowl. Line the colander with several layers of cheesecloth and pour rhubarb mixture into it. Let the juice drain through undisturbed for about 12 hours or until the mixture stops dripping, then measure the juice. Add water, if needed, to make 2 cups liquid. Combine the juice and sugar in a large saucepan. Stir over moderate heat until the sugar dissolves and the mixture comes to a boil. Stir in the liquid pectin all at once and bring to a full rolling boil, stirring constantly. Boil hard for 1 minute. Remove from heat. Skim off foam quickly and ladle into hot jelly glasses or jelly jars. Fill the glasses to within 1/2 inch of top and jars to within 1/8 inch of top. Seal the glasses with paraffin and the jars with lids. Four 6-ounce glasses or three 8-ounce jars.

Parsley Jelly (page 96); Cranberry Jelly (page 96); Rhubarb-Strawberry Jelly (above)

LOQUAT JELLY

Hard, partially ripe loquats   **Sugar**

Wash the loquats and remove the blossom ends. Barely cover the loquats with water and bring to a boil. Simmer until soft and pour into a jelly bag to strain the juice. Bring the juice to a boil and simmer until thick and red. Measure the juice and add 1 cup sugar per cup juice. Boil over high heat to the jelly stage. Pour into hot sterilized jars or jelly glasses and seal.

Mrs. Chris Hobbs, Gallup, New Mexico

MINT JELLY

Tart, firm apples   **Sugar**
1 c. (firmly packed) mint   **Green food coloring**
  leaves

Wash the apples thoroughly and remove the stems. Slice the apples and place in a large kettle. Add about half as much water as apples and bring to a boil. Simmer until the apples are soft. Turn the fruit and juice into a jelly bag and let the juice drip into a container below. Pour 1 cup boiling water over the mint leaves and let stand for 1 hour. Press the juice from the leaves. Measure the apple juice and add 2 tablespoons of the mint juice to each cup of apple juice. Bring to a boil, then add 3/4 cup sugar for each cup juice. Stir to dissolve the sugar and boil over high heat to the jelly stage. Add the food coloring to desired tint and pour the jelly into hot jelly glasses. Pour in about 1/8 inch hot paraffin and allow to cool. Cover with lids.

Mrs. Fay Elmore, Richmond, Virginia

ORANGE-LEMON JELLY

Juice of 12 lemons   **Sugar**
12 oranges, sliced

Measure the lemon juice and add 3 cups water for each cup lemon juice. Add the orange slices and let stand for 12 hours. Bring the orange mixture to a boil and boil until the oranges are tender. Strain the juice through a cloth or a jelly bag. Measure the juice, then bring to a boil. Add 1 3/4 cups sugar to each 2 cups juice, stirring to dissolve. Boil over high heat until the jelly sheets from a spoon. Pour into hot sterilized jelly glasses or jars and seal.

Ginger Hill, Houston, Texas

PEACH JELLY

3 1/2 lb. ripe peaches   **4 1/2 c. sugar**
1 box powdered pectin

Peel the peaches and remove the stones. Crush in a large kettle. Add 1 cup water and simmer, covered, for 10 minutes. Place in a jelly bag and squeeze out the juice. Combine the pectin with 3 1/2 cups peach juice in the kettle. Cook and stir over high heat until mixture comes to a hard boil. Stir in the sugar and bring to a rolling boil. Boil for 1 minute, stirring constantly. Remove jelly from heat and skim off foam. Pour into sterilized jars immediately, leaving 1/2-inch space at top. Seal with lids.

Mrs. Rollen Bishop, Purlear, North Carolina

PINEAPPLE JELLY

1 fresh pineapple	**Sugar**
Tart apple juice	

Peel and core the pineapple and chop the flesh. Cover the pineapple partially with water, then bring to a boil and simmer until tender. Pour the flesh and juice into a jelly bag and strain. Measure the pineapple juice and add an equal amount of apple juice. Add 3 cups sugar for each 2 cups juice. Stir to mix well, then boil over high heat until the liquid sheets from a spoon. Pour immediately into hot sterilized glasses and seal.

Mrs. Nancy Shelton, Orlando, Florida

POMEGRANATE JELLY

10 med. pomegranates	**Food coloring**
Sugar	

Remove the pomegranate pulp from rinds. Combine 1/2 cup water and the pulp in a large saucepan. Place over low heat and boil for 15 minutes. Pour pulp in a jelly bag and let drain. Add 1 cup sugar to each cup juice. Add 3/4 cup sugar to each cup juice if using sweet pomegranates. Pour in a large saucepan and add food coloring. Boil rapidly until jelly sheets from a spoon. Pour in sterilized jars and cover tightly.

Mrs. John H. Green, Transylvania, Louisiana

PRICKLY PEAR JELLY

Prickly pears	**6 c. sugar**
4 c. cactus juice	**1/8 tsp. salt**
1/2 c. lemon juice	**1 1/2 pkg. pectin**

Use kitchen tongs to gather cactus fruit. Select several green pears with the ripe pears. Wash the fruit with a hard spray then place in a large pan with water to almost cover. Cook for 10 minutes and mash with a potato masher and cook for 10 minutes longer. Strain as for any other juice for jelly. Pour the cactus juice and lemon juice in a large pan and bring to a boil. Add sugar and salt, all at once and bring to a boil, stirring constantly. Boil for 3 minutes. Remove from heat and stir in the pectin, then skim. Pour into sterilized jelly glasses and cover with melted paraffin. 5-6 glasses.

Emma Catherine Lawson, Carrizozo, New Mexico

QUINCE JELLY

Quinces   Sugar
Orange juice

Wash the quinces thoroughly. Cut in fourths and discard the cores. Add water to almost cover and bring to a boil. Simmer for about 45 minutes or until tender. Strain the juice through a cloth or a jelly bag, then measure and add an equal amount of orange juice. Bring to a boil and reduce the heat. Simmer for about 20 minutes, then stir in 3/4 cup sugar per cup juice. Boil over high heat until the liquid sheets from a spoon.

Mrs. Vivian Beck, Albany, Georgia

APRICOT MARMALADE

2 lb. dried apricots   3/4 c. lemon juice
12 oranges   1 3/4 c. crushed pineapple
1 grapefruit   Sugar

Soak the apricots in water to cover overnight. Peel the oranges and grapefruit and remove the white rind. Cut the apricots, oranges and grapefruit in pieces and add the lemon juice and pineapple. Measure the combined fruits and add an equal amount of sugar. Cook, stirring carefully, until thick. Fill sterilized glasses to 1/2 inch from the top and seal.

Mrs. Margaret Andrews, Baton Rouge, Louisiana

BANANA MARMALADE

3 lb. firm ripe bananas   5 c. sugar
Juice and grated rind of   Grated rind of 1/2 orange
    2 lemons

Peel and slice the bananas into rounds. Cut out any dark spots. Combine all the ingredients in a large kettle. Cook over low heat, stirring until the sugar dissolves. Cook, stirring frequently to prevent sticking, for about 15 minutes or until the mixture is of desired consistency. Pour into sterilized jars and seal. Store banana marmalade in a cool place.

Mrs. Mary Gates, Miami, Florida

EASY CARROT MARMALADE

1 orange, ground   3 c. ground carrots
1 1/2 to 2 lemons, ground   3 c. sugar

Mix the orange, lemons and carrots. Add water to cover and simmer until tender. Add the sugar. Simmer, stirring often, until the mixture sheets from a spoon. Pour into hot jars and seal.

Holly Schrank, Nashville, Tennessee

GREEN TOMATO MARMALADE

4 lb. green tomatoes	4 c. sugar
3 lemons, thinly sliced	1/2 tsp. salt

Core the tomatoes and cut into small pieces. Cook the lemons in a small amount of water until tender. Combine the tomatoes, lemons and remaining ingredients. Cook and stir over low heat until the sugar is dissolved. Boil until the tomatoes are soft. Pour into hot pint jars and fit with lids. Process in boiling water in a waterbath canner for 10 minutes.

Mrs. Maud Vernon, Asheville, North Carolina

PARTY CARROT MARMALADE

2 oranges	1 sm. piece of gingerroot
3 c. grated carrots	Juice of 3 lemons
4 c. sugar	1/2 tsp. salt

Wash and peel the oranges, then grind in a food grinder. Combine the ground oranges and 1 cup water in a saucepan and cook until tender. Put the grated carrots through the food grinder, then cook in a small amount of water until tender and drain well. Blend the sugar, hot carrots, orange pulp and peel, gingerroot, lemon juice and salt. Boil over low heat, stirring frequently, until the marmalade is thick and very syrupy. Ladle immediately into hot jelly or canning jars. Fill to within 1/8 inch of tops and screw caps on evenly and tightly. Invert for several seconds and stand jars upright to cool. Six 8-ounce jars or about 3 pints.

Party Carrot Marmalade (above), Strawberry and Rhubarb Marmalade (page 107)

101

CANTALOUPE MARMALADE

4 c. cubed ripe cantaloupe   **3 c. sugar**
Juice and grated rind of 1 lemon

Place the cantaloupe in a bowl and add the lemon juice and rind. Pour the sugar over the top and let stand overnight. Transfer to a large kettle and cook over low heat, stirring frequently, until thick. Let cool to room temperature, then stir to keep the fruits evenly distributed. Pour in hot sterilized glasses and cover with 1/8 inch hot paraffin.

GRAPEFRUIT-ORANGE MARMALADE

1 grapefruit   **6 oranges**
2 lemons   **14 c. sugar**

Cut the fruits in half and discard the seeds. Cut in thin slices, then cover with cold water and let stand for about 12 hours. Cook over low heat to boiling point. Turn the heat to high and boil until the peel is tender. Add the sugar and boil until the liquid sheets from a spoon. Cool slightly and pack in hot jars. Adjust the jar lids. Process in boiling water in a waterbath canner for 10 minutes.

Mrs. Barbara Dean, Houston, Texas

ORANGE-RHUBARB MARMALADE

3 med. oranges, ground   **1 qt. cut rhubarb**
5 c. sugar

Mix the oranges and sugar in a saucepan and boil for 5 minutes. Add the rhubarb and cook for 20 to 25 minutes or until thick, stirring frequently. Pour into sterilized jars and seal.

Mrs. Henrietta Lyons, Brookhaven, Mississippi

KUMQUAT MARMALADE

12 kumquats   **1/4 c. lemon juice**
1 orange   **Sugar**

Wash the kumquats thoroughly and drain. Slice as thin as possible and discard the seed. Cut the orange in eighths, discarding the seed, then chop. Measure the kumquats and orange and add 3 cups water per cup fruit. Let stand overnight in a cool place. Bring to a boil and reduce the heat. Simmer until the peel is tender. Measure the kumquat mixture and add the lemon juice and 1 cup sugar for each cup mixture. Boil until the liquid sheets from a spoon, then pour into hot sterilized jars and seal.

Mrs. Drucilla Hawthorne, Macon, Georgia

LIME MARMALADE

6 sm. limes   **Sugar**
3 lemons

Scrub the limes and lemons, then cut in halves and remove the seed. Cut into thin slices. Measure the fruits and juice and add 3 times the amount of water. Soak for 12 hours. Simmer for 20 minutes, then let stand for 12 hours. Add 3/4 cup sugar for every cup of fruit and juice. Cook the mixture until jellying stage is reached. Pour into sterilized jars, leaving 1/4-inch margin at top and cover with melted paraffin. Cool on a metal rack and store in a cool dry place. 3 jelly glasses.

Anne Morrison Smith, Jesup, Georgia

OLD-FASHIONED MELON MARMALADE

2 honeydew melons   **3 lemons**
4 lb. sugar   **1 sm. pineapple**

Peel the melons and cut in chunks. Discard the seed and stringy substance. Add the sugar and let stand for about 12 hours. Cut the lemons in quarters and discard the seed. Peel the pineapple and cut in chunks. Put the lemons and the pineapple through the food grinder, using the coarse blade. Combine the ground fruits and melons in a large kettle and bring to a boil over low heat, stirring frequently. Simmer until the melons are transparent and the juice is almost to the jellying stage. Spoon into hot sterilized jars and seal.

ORANGE MARMALADE

6 lge. oranges	2 tbsp. lemon juice
Sugar	

Wash the oranges thoroughly, then cut in halves. Trim off the stem ends and remove the seeds. Cut into thin strips and measure. Add 2 cups water for each cup fruit and soak overnight. Bring the orange mixture to a boil, then reduce the heat. Simmer until tender, then add 1 cup sugar for each cup orange mixture. Add the lemon juice and cook, stirring to dissolve the sugar and to prevent sticking, until of the consistency of marmalade. Remove from heat and stir for about 5 minutes to prevent the orange strips from floating on the top. Pour into sterilized glasses and seal.

Mrs. Shirley Farrell, Orlando, Florida

PEAR MARMALADE

8 lb. firm cooking pears	1 2-oz. jar candied ginger
4 lge. oranges	5 lb. sugar
2 lge. lemons	

Cut the pears in quarters, then pare and remove the core. Cut the oranges and lemons in quarters and remove the seed. Put the pears, oranges, lemons and candied ginger through the coarse blade of a food chopper. About 2 quarts ground pears and 1 quart ground oranges and lemons should be the result. Place the ground fruits and ginger in a large kettle, then add the sugar. Place over moderate heat and bring to a boil, stirring frequently. Boil gently for 30 to 45 minutes, stirring frequently or until the fruit is translucent and the syrup sheets from a spoon. Remove from heat. Skim off the foam quickly and ladle immediately into hot jelly jars or canning jars. Fill to within 1/8 inch of top, then screw the cap on evenly and tightly. Invert for several seconds and stand jars upright to cool. Fourteen 8-ounce jars or 7 pints.

Photograph for this recipe on page 2.

TOMATO MARMALADE

3 oranges	6 c. sugar
2 lemons	1 tsp. salt
2 c. water	6 cinnamon sticks
3 qt. sliced peeled ripe	1 tbsp. whole cloves
tomatoes	6 whole allspice

Remove the outer rind from the oranges and lemons with a vegetable peeler, then cut into thin slivers with a knife or scissors. Place in a saucepan, then add the water and simmer, covered, for 15 minutes. Drain and reserve the rind. Peel the oranges and lemons, then remove the seed and cut into small pieces. Combine the tomatoes, sugar, salt, cooked rind and cut-up oranges and lemons in a large heavy kettle and mix lightly. Tie the cinnamon sticks, cloves and allspice in several layers of cheese cloth and add to the tomato mixture. Bring to a boil over low heat, stirring almost constantly. Boil over low heat, stirring almost constantly, for 1 hour or until marmalade is thick and syrupy. Remove from heat and remove the spices. Ladle immediately into hot jelly jars or canning jars. Fill to within 1/8 inch of top and screw caps on evenly and tightly. Invert for several seconds and stand jars upright to cool. Eight to nine 8-ounce jars or about 4 pints.

Photograph for this recipe on page 2.

BLUEBERRY MARMALADE

1 lemon   **7 c. sugar**
4 pt. blueberries

Peel the lemon with a sharp knife, then cut the peel in thin strips. Soak the peel overnight in water, then simmer for about 30 minutes or until almost soft. Add about 2 tablespoons lemon juice, the blueberries and sugar to the lemon peel. Cook over low heat, stirring frequently, until the juice will run off the spoon in 2 drops or until almost to the jellying point. Remove from heat and let cool to room temperature. Stir to keep the blueberries and peel distributed, then ladle into jelly glasses or jars and seal.

Blueberry Marmalade (above)

105

MYSTERY MARMALADE

2 c. finely chopped cucumbers	Few drops of green food
4 c. sugar	coloring
1/2 c. lime juice	1/2 c. fruit pectin
2 tbsp. grated lime peel	

Place the cucumbers in a large saucepan, then add the sugar, lime juice and peel. Mix well. Place over high heat and add food coloring. Bring to a rolling boil and boil for exactly 1 minute, stirring constantly. Remove from heat and stir in pectin immediately. Skim off foam. Cool for 5 minutes, stirring and skimming. Ladle quickly into sterilized glasses and cover with 1/4 inch hot paraffin. 5 medium glasses.

Mrs. L. C. Martinez, El Paso, Texas

ORANGE-PINEAPPLE MARMALADE

6 oranges	1 fresh pineapple
1 lemon	Sugar

Wash the oranges and lemon and cut in quarters. Remove and discard the seed, then force the rind and pulp through a food chopper. Weigh the chopped fruit and add 1 quart water per pound fruit. Bring to a boil and simmer for 1 hour. Let stand for 20 minutes. Peel and core the pineapple, then grate or finely chop the flesh. Add the pineapple to the cooked fruit and cook until the pineapple is tender. Allow to cool and weigh the combined fruits. Add an equal amount of sugar and bring to a boil, stirring to dissolve the sugar. Boil over high heat until the marmalade is of desired thickness. Pack immediately into hot jars and seal.

Mrs. Anita Horn, Roswell, New Mexico

PEACH MARMALADE

12 peaches	Sugar
2 oranges	1 c. maraschino cherry halves

Peel the peaches and remove the stones, then cut into thin slices. Grate the orange rind, then remove the white membrane and seeds. Slice and chop the orange sections, reserving the juice. Measure the peach slices, orange rind, juice and pulp and add an equal amount of sugar. Add the cherries and cook over low heat, stirring frequently, until thick. Pour in hot sterilized jars and seal. 5-6 pints.

Mrs. Glenda Ballinger, Chattanooga, Tennessee

PRICKLY PEAR MARMALADE

4 c. chopped prickly pears	2 oranges
1 c. sliced lemon	Sugar

Wash the pears and lemon. Cut the lemon into paper thin slices. Measure. Chop the orange peel and pulp. Add 4 cups water to the lemon and orange mixture. Let stand for 12 hours in a cool place. Bring to a boil and boil until the peel is tender. Cool. Pare, chop and measure the pears. Measure the lemon, orange and cooking liquid. Add 1 cup sugar for each cup pears and lemon mixture. Boil to the jellying point. Pour into hot jars and seal.

Mrs. Linda Adams, Tempe, Arizona

SEVEN-FRUIT MARMALADE

1 grapefruit	1 No. 2 can crushed pineapple
12 kumquats	1 5-oz. bottle maraschino
1 lemon	cherries, chopped
4 oranges	Sugar
12 calamondins	

Cut the first 5 fruits in half and remove the seeds, then force through a grinder. Measure the fruits. Add 2 cups water to each cup fruit. Let stand overnight, then cook until tender. Add the crushed pineapple and cherries. Add 7/8 cup sugar for each cup fruit. Cook to 222 degrees or until syrup sheets from a spoon. Pack into hot sterilized jars and seal.

Mrs. John F. Lawrence, Largo, Florida

TANGERINE MARMALADE

6 tangerines	Juice of 2 1/2 lemons
3 1/2 c. sugar	

Wash the tangerines thoroughly, then peel. Cut the peel into shreds. Remove the stringy substance and seed. Mash the tangerine segments in a Dutch oven and add 3 1/2 cups water. Let stand for about 12 hours. Bring the tangerine mixture to a boil and simmer until the peel is tender. Add the sugar, then cook and stir until the sugar is dissolved. Add the lemon juice and bring to a boil over high heat. Boil for about 20 minutes, stirring frequently to prevent sticking. Remove from heat and stir for several minutes to prevent the peel from floating to the surface. Pour into hot sterilized glasses and seal. About 6 half-pints.

Mrs. Billie Allen, Clearwater, Florida

STRAWBERRY AND RHUBARB MARMALADE

5 c. diced rhubarb	2 c. sugar
1 qt. strawberries	

Place the rhubarb, strawberries and sugar in a kettle and let stand until sugar is moistened by fruit juices. Simmer for 20 minutes or until the mixture sheets from a spoon. Pour into sterilized half-pint glasses. Cool until firm and seal with melted paraffin. 8-10 glasses.

Photograph for this recipe on page 101.

conserves and preserves

Conserves and preserves are depended upon in hundreds of southern homes to provide accompaniments to the main course or for desserts. Conserves are combinations of foods that usually contain raisins and nuts; preserves are whole fruits that have been canned in a syrup.

Recipes for these two foods are shared with you in the pages that follow. The first one you'll find is a recipe for Ambrosia Conserve, a blend of citrus and tart fruits with raisins and coconut. This has long been a traditional southern dessert — with cans of homemade ambrosia preserves on your shelves, you too can serve your family this tangy finish to a meal. Ambrosia Conserve is followed by recipes for All Fruit Conserve . . . Apple-Blueberry Conserve . . . and Christmas Conserve, a tart blend of oranges, cranberries, raisins, and nuts.

Preserves, too, can serve as accompaniments or desserts. Beginning with Apple Chutney, a complement to curries, poultry, or seafood, you'll find page after page of recipes for Fig Preserves, a traditional southern dish . . . Peach Preserves, another favorite in the Southland . . . Watermelon Rind Preserves . . . Southern Cinnamon-Pumpkin Preserves . . . and other, equally delicious preserves.

For conserves and preserves that you'll serve with pride — and have fun preparing — choose one of the recipes in this section. They're home-tested, your guarantee of success!

AMBROSIA CONSERVE

2 med. oranges
1 lge. ripe pineapple
6 cooking apples
2 c. water

1 c. raisins
6 c. sugar
1 3 1/2-oz. can flaked
    coconut

Remove the outer rind of the oranges with a vegetable peeler and cut with a knife or scissors into thin slivers. Cut off the remaining peel from the oranges and remove the seed, then cut into small pieces. Peel the pineapple and cut in small cubes. Pare, core and chop the apples. Combine the orange rind and pulp, pineapple, chopped apples and water in a large kettle. Bring to a boil. Reduce the heat and simmer, covered, for 10 minutes. Add the raisins and sugar and stir over moderate heat until the sugar dissolves. Add the coconut and boil rapidly for 20 to 30 minutes, stirring almost constantly, until the mixture sheets from a spoon. Remove from heat. Skim off foam quickly and ladle immediately into hot jelly jars or canning jars. Fill to within 1/8 inch of tops and screw caps on evenly and tightly. Invert for several seconds and stand jars upright to cool. Eight 8-ounce jars or 4 pints.

Photograph for this recipe on page 108.

APRICOT CONSERVE

1/4 lb. dried apricots
1 No. 1 can crushed pineapple
1/4 c. raisins
1/2 c. chopped pecans

Juice and grated rind of 1/2
    lemon
1 1/2 c. sugar

Wash the apricots and drain. Cover with 1 3/4 cups water and soak for several hours. Cook until soft and tender, then mash to a pulp. Drain the pineapple and combine the pineapple juice with enough water to make 1/4 cup liquid. Add the fruits, pecans, lemon juice and rind, sugar and pineapple liquid to the apricots. Cook for 10 to 20 minutes, stirring frequently, then pour into sterilized glasses and seal.

Beadie L. Kilpatrick, Temple, Texas

BLUEBERRY CONSERVE

4 c. sugar
1/2 c. raisins
1/2 lemon, thinly sliced

1/2 orange, thinly sliced
4 c. blueberries

Combine the sugar and 2 cups water in a large kettle and bring to a boil. Add the raisins, lemon and orange slices and simmer for about 5 minutes. Add the blueberries and cook over low heat, stirring to prevent sticking, until the liquid sheets from a spoon. Pour into hot sterilized jars and seal.

Mrs. Cherry Dunn, Owensboro, Kentucky

CALIFORNIA CONSERVE

1 orange	1 1 3/4-oz. package
2 lemons	powdered fruit pectin
1 lb. dried figs	5 c. sugar
2 c. water	1 3 1/2-oz. can flaked coconut

Slice the orange and lemons paper-thin, then cut each slice into quarters. Slice the figs. Combine the orange, lemons, figs and water in a large kettle and bring to a boil. Cover and simmer for 30 minutes. Add the pectin and mix well. Cook over high heat, stirring, until mixture comes to a boil, then stir in sugar immediately. Bring to a boil and boil for 1 minute, stirring constantly. Remove from heat and add the coconut. Ladle into scalded jelly glasses and seal. Ten 6-ounce glasses.

Mrs. Essie Hargrove, Houston, Texas

ALL FRUIT CONSERVE

2 lge. oranges	4 lge. ripe peaches
2 lge. lemons	7 c. sugar
4 c. fresh strawberries	3 c. chopped walnuts
2 c. diced fresh pineapple	

Cut the oranges and lemons in eighths and discard the seeds. Place in a blender container with the strawberries and pineapple. Peel, halve and pit the peaches, then add to the blender container. Cover and chop all the fruits. Pour into heavy kettle and add the sugar. Cook and stir over low heat until the sugar is dissolved. Bring to a boil and cook, stirring frequently, until thick and clear. Stir in the walnuts. Spoon into hot sterilized jars and seal.

Special Apple Conserve (below)

SPECIAL APPLE CONSERVE

4 c. canned applesauce	1 c. sugar
1 c. chopped dried apricots	2 tbsp. lemon juice
1 1-lb. 4 1/2-oz. can	3/4 c. raisins
crushed pineapple, drained	

Combine all ingredients in a saucepan and simmer for 30 minutes, stirring frequently. Spoon into hot sterilized 1/2-pint jars, leaving 1/2-inch head space. Seal. Serve with meat or poultry.

APPLE-BLUEBERRY CONSERVE

4 c. chopped apples	1/2 c. raisins
4 c. blueberries	4 tbsp. lemon juice
6 c. sugar	

Combine all the ingredients in a heavy kettle. Cook over low heat, stirring, until the sugar dissolves, then boil until thick. Pour into hot sterilized jars and seal.

Mrs. Susanne Anderson, Wheeling, West Virginia

APPLE-PINEAPPLE CONSERVE

2 oranges	1 1/2 c. grated coconut
4 c. diced apples	6 c. sugar
4 c. chopped pineapple	

Slice the peel of 1 orange thin. Remove the pulp from both oranges and cut in small pieces. Combine the orange peel and pulp, apples and pineapple in a large kettle and add 3 cups water. Boil until the peel is tender. Add the coconut and sugar and boil almost to the jellying point. Pour immediately into hot sterilized jars and seal.

Photograph for this recipe on page 147.

BLACK CHERRY CONSERVE

2 oranges, thinly sliced	Juice of 1 lemon
4 c. pitted black cherries	1 c. slivered almonds
3 1/2 c. sugar	

Cover the orange slices with water and bring to a boil. Boil until soft. Add remaining ingredients except the almonds and boil until thick and clear. Add the almonds and boil for 2 minutes. Pour into hot sterilized jars and seal.

Mrs. Beulah Connor, Greenville, Mississippi

CARROT CONSERVE

1 qt. carrots, scraped	1/2 tsp. salt
2 lge. oranges	2 lb. sugar
Juice of 3 lemons	1/2 c. broken blanched almonds

Force the carrots and orange rind through a food chopper. Cover with water and cook over high heat until tender. Add the lemon juice, orange pulp and salt and cook until thick. Add the sugar and boil over high heat until thick and clear. Add the almonds and pour into sterilized glasses. Seal.

Mrs. Frances T. Swaringen, Oakboro, North Carolina

CHRISTMAS CONSERVE

2 oranges	1 c. raisins
4 c. cranberries	1/4 tsp. salt
3 c. sugar	1/2 c. chopped nutmeats

Grate the rind of the oranges and remove the white membrane from the pulp. Cut the pulp in small pieces. Add 2 cups water to the peel and pulp and cook for 20 minutes. Add remaining ingredients except the nutmeats and boil over high heat to the jelly stage. Add the nutmeats and boil for 5 minutes longer. Pour into hot jars and seal.

Mrs. Beatrice Harp, Laurel, Mississippi

*(Clockwise) Orange Conserve (below); Spiced Oranges (page 20);
Orange-Apricot Conserve (below)*

ORANGE CONSERVE

6 Florida oranges	4 tbsp. Florida lime
5 c. water	juice or vinegar
6 c. sugar	1/2 c. ground raisins
1 2-in. stick cinnamon	1/2 c. chopped nuts

Remove the orange peel in quarters, using the point of a paring knife. Dice the pulp, removing the center membrane and seeds. Grind the peel through a food chopper, using the coarse blade. Cover the peel with water and bring to a boil, then cook for about 20 minutes or until peel is tender. Add the pulp and juice to the rind and cook for about 20 minutes or until mixture is reduced by one-half. Add the sugar, cinnamon, lime juice, and raisins and stir until the sugar is dissolved. Cook for about 30 minutes or until syrup runs off side of spoon in 2 drops which sheet together. Stir in the nuts. Pour into hot sterilized jars or glasses and seal with paraffin at once. Seven 8-ounce glasses.

ORANGE-APRICOT CONSERVE

1 1/2 c. orange juice	2 tbsp. lemon juice
3 1/2 c. canned unpeeled	3 1/2 c. sugar
apricots	1/2 c. chopped nuts
1/2 c. shredded orange peel	

Combine the first 5 ingredients in a large kettle and cook until thick, stirring constantly. Add the nuts and stir to mix well. Remove from heat. Cool for 5 minutes, stirring and skimming. Pour into hot sterilized glasses and seal.

Mrs. Norman King, Glendale, West Virginia

CHERRY-APPLE-PINEAPPLE CONSERVE

8 c. pitted cherries	11 c. sugar
3 c. chopped apples	1/2 tsp. salt
2 c. chopped pineapple	1 c. chopped nuts

Combine the fruits and sugar and mix well. Let stand for 4 to 5 hours. Boil until the liquid is almost to the jellying point, then add the salt and nuts. Cook for about 5 minutes longer. Pour boiling conserve into hot sterilized jars and seal.

Mrs. Arlene Marshall, Miami, Florida

CHERRY-PINEAPPLE CONSERVE

1 c. Surinam cherries, pitted	1 tbsp. lime juice
1 c. grated fresh pineapple, drained	1 tbsp. lemon juice
1 c. orange juice	1 2/3 c. sugar

Combine all the ingredients in a saucepan and cook over medium heat until mixture begins to thicken. Pour into sterilized jars and seal. 4 4-ounce jars.

Mrs. Susan Kelly, Miami, Florida

PEAR-MUSCADINE CONSERVE

4 c. coarsely-ground pears	Sugar
2 c. muscadine juice	1 c. chopped pecans

Combine the pears and juice in a large saucepan and cook until the pears are tender. Measure and add an equal amount of sugar. Cook over high heat until the liquid sheets from a spoon, then add the pecans and simmer for 5 minutes. Pour immediately into hot sterilized jars and seal.

Mrs. Joan Barnett, Montgomery, Alabama

PEAR CONSERVE

3 c. peeled sliced pears	1 c. seedless raisins
2 1/2 c. sugar	Juice of 1 lemon
1 orange	1 c. chopped nuts

Combine the pears and sugar and let stand overnight. Cut the orange in half and extract the juice. Remove and chop half the peel. Combine the pear mixture, orange peel, raisins and juices. Cook for about 30 minutes, then add the nuts and cook for 5 minutes longer. Pour into sterilized jars and seal while hot. 2 pints.

Mrs. Charles Yount, Catawba, North Carolina

FIG CONSERVE

2 lb. fresh figs
3 tbsp. soda
1/2 lb. raisins
1 orange

3 c. sugar
Juice of 1 lemon
1/2 c. chopped pecans

Sprinkle the figs with the soda, then add about 1 quart boiling water. Let stand for 5 minutes, then drain and rinse thoroughly. Cut the figs and raisins in small pieces. Peel the orange and cut the peel in shreds. Remove the white membrane and cut the pulp in small pieces. Combine the fruits, sugar and juice in a large kettle and cook until thick and clear. Add the pecans and mix well. Pour into hot sterilized jars and seal.

Mrs. Carol Hinkle, Nashville, Tennessee

FRUIT SALAD CONSERVE

1 lb. seedless white grapes
1 c. red plums
4 lb. ripe peaches
1 orange, thinly sliced

1 c. pineapple juice
1 c. pineapple tidbits
Sugar

Cut the grapes in halves. Pit and dice the plums. Plunge the peaches in hot water until the skins slip, then peel and slice. Combine the peaches, grapes, plums and the orange in a large kettle and add the juice. Bring to a boil and reduce the heat. Simmer, stirring frequently, for about 30 minutes. Measure the cooked fruit and the pineapple and add 3/4 cup sugar for each cup fruit. Bring to a boil, then simmer, stirring to prevent sticking, until the liquid sheets from a spoon. Pour into hot jars and seal.

Mrs. Juanita Finley, Greenville, South Carolina

GRAPE CONSERVE

1 lb. grapes
1/4 orange, seeds removed
1/4 c. seedless raisins

1 c. sugar
1/4 tsp. salt
1/4 c. chopped nuts

Wash the grapes thoroughly, then drain and remove the stems. Separate the skins and the pulp. Chop the skins and reserve. Cook the grape pulp for about 10 minutes, then press through a food mill and discard the seeds. Chop the orange, using the fine blade in the food chopper. Combine the grape pulp, orange, raisins, sugar and salt in a large kettle. Cook, stirring frequently, over high heat until slightly thickened, then add the reserved grape skins and cook for about 10 minutes. Stir in the nuts and pour immediately into hot jars. Fasten lids and process in boiling water in a waterbath canner for 10 minutes.

Mrs. Sara Grant, Augusta, Georgia

PEACH-CANTALOUPE CONSERVE

4 c. chopped peeled cantaloupe	1/2 tsp. nutmeg
4 c. chopped peeled peaches	1/4 tsp. salt
6 c. sugar	1 tsp. grated lemon peel
1/4 c. lemon juice	1/2 c. chopped walnuts

Combine the cantaloupe and peaches in a large heavy saucepan. Simmer for 20 minutes, stirring until enough liquid collects to prevent fruit from sticking. Add remaining ingredients except walnuts and cook, stirring frequently, until thick. Add the walnuts and boil for 3 minutes. Ladle into hot jars and seal. 4-5 half-pints.

Mrs. Mary Ann Block, Knoxville, Tennessee

PEACH CONSERVE

1 lge. tart seedless orange	1/2 tsp. salt
7 c. 1/2-in. peach chunks	1/4 tsp. ground ginger
5 1/2 c. sugar	1/4 tsp. nutmeg
1 c. small pineapple chunks	

Remove the thin yellow part of orange peel with a sharp knife, then cut the orange in paper thin slices. Cut the slices in 1/8 to 1/4-inch wedges. Place in kettle and add cold water to just cover. Cook over low heat until peel is soft. Add the remaining ingredients, then bring to a boil and boil rapidly, stirring frequently, until fruit is translucent. Remove the foam and pour quickly into hot sterilized jars to 1/8 inch of top of jar. Wipe off anything spilled on top or threads of jar. Put dome lid on jar; screw band or cap tight.

Photographs for this recipe below and on page 12.

Peach Conserve (above)

QUICK PEACH CONSERVE

4 lb. ripe freestone peaches	1 No. 2 1/2 can crushed
1 sm. jar maraschino cherries	pineapple
1/2 c. frozen orange juice	6 c. sugar
Juice of 2 lemons	1 pkg. fruit pectin

Peel and slice the peaches. Drain and coarsely chop the cherries. Combine all the ingredients except the pectin. Cook, stirring frequently, over low heat until the peaches are clear, then add the pectin. Bring to a boil and boil for 1 minute. Pour into hot sterilized jars and seal with paraffin. 10 glasses.

Ruth Jeffers, Estancia, New Mexico

GOOSEBERRY CONSERVE

4 c. gooseberries	1 c. raisins
1 orange	1/2 c. chopped nuts
2 2/3 c. sugar	

Wash and drain the gooseberries. Grate the orange rind, then remove the white membrane. Cut the pulp in small pieces. Mix the gooseberries, orange rind and pulp, sugar and raisins. Cook over low heat and stir until the sugar dissolves, then boil over high heat until the liquid sheets from a spoon. Add the nuts and stir to mix well. Pour immediately into hot jars and seal.

Mrs. Ginny Lamar, Asheville, North Carolina

MANGO-APRICOT CONSERVE

2 lb. firm, ripe mangoes	1 1/2 c. drained canned
2 c. sugar	apricots
1/4 c. lemon juice	

Peel and dice the mangoes. Combine with sugar and lemon juice and cook over medium heat for about 15 minutes or until thick. Add the apricots and bring to a boil. Pour into hot sterilized jars and seal. 2 pints.

Dorothy Zill, Boynton Beach, Florida

CONSERVE DELIGHT

6 c. sliced fresh peaches	2 lemons, skinned, seeded and
3 c. white seedless grapes,	diced
halved	1 c. orange juice
2 c. diced pineapple	9 c. sugar
2 c. peeled diced red plums	

Combine all the ingredients and let stand for several hours or overnight. Cook 1/3 of the mixture at a time until thickened. Pour into sterilized jars and seal. 7 pints.

Mrs. Marjorie Hall, Winston, Kentucky

PINEAPPLE CONSERVE

1 qt. chopped pineapple pulp, undrained	1 lemon
2 oranges	3 c. sugar

Cook pineapple until tender. Grate the rinds of the oranges and the lemon. Remove the pulp from the membrane. Combine the pineapple, orange and lemon rinds and pulp and the sugar. Cook, stirring frequently, over high heat until the pineapple mixture is thick. Pour into sterilized glasses and seal.

Mrs. Rita Tilton, Jacksonville, Florida

PLUM CONSERVE

3 lb. sliced damson plums	1 lb. seeded raisins
1 1/2 lb. sugar	1 orange, thinly sliced
1 lemon, thinly sliced	1 c. chopped walnuts

Combine the plums, sugar, lemon, raisins and orange with a small amount of water in a heavy kettle and cook until thick and clear, then add the nuts. Pour into hot sterilized glasses. Cool and cover with melted paraffin to seal. 4 pints.

Mary Ella Crozier, Elgin, Texas

PRUNE CONSERVE

3 lb. prunes	3 lb. sugar
3 oranges	1/2 lb. broken walnuts

Pit and cut up the prunes. Grate the rind of 1 orange, then combine with the prunes, pulp and juice of all the oranges. Add 1 1/2 pounds sugar and mix, then let stand for 24 hours. Cook until clear, then add remaining sugar and cook until thick. Add the walnuts and bring to a boil. Pour into hot jars and seal.

Mrs. Hazel M. Palmer, Montgomery, Alabama

RHUBARB CONSERVE

2 lge. oranges, thinly sliced	3 c. red currants, stemmed
2 lge. lemons, thinly sliced	3 c. seedless raisins, chopped
7 1/2 c. cut-up rhubarb	10 c. sugar
4 c. fresh red raspberries	4 c. chopped walnuts

Combine the oranges, lemons, rhubarb, raspberries, currants, raisins and sugar in a heavy kettle. Cook over low heat, stirring constantly, to the boiling point. Cook for about 30 minutes or until thick as jam. Remove from heat and stir in the walnuts. Pour into hot sterilized glasses and seal.

Mrs. Hope Halliday, Lawton, Oklahoma

RHUBARB-STRAWBERRY CONSERVE

4 c. cut rhubarb	7 c. sugar
4 c. strawberries	

Combine all the ingredients in a large kettle and cook over low heat, stirring to dissolve the sugar. Boil over high heat until thickened. Pour hot conserve into hot sterilized jars and seal.

Mrs. Teresa Billings, Dundalk, Maryland

STRAWBERRY CONSERVE

1 c. ground cherries	1 c. freshly ground pineapple
3 c. strawberries	5 c. sugar

Combine all the ingredients and mix well. Cook, stirring to prevent sticking, until thick, then pour in sterilized jars and seal.

Mrs. Johnathan Barker, Harrodsburg, Kentucky

TUTTI-FRUTTI CONSERVE

3 c. chopped pears	1/2 c. lemon juice
1 lge. orange, seeded and chopped	1/2 c. chopped nuts
	1 c. coconut
1/2 c. maraschino cherries	5 c. sugar
3/4 c. drained crushed pineapple	1 pkg. powdered pectin

Mix the pears, orange, cherries, pineapple, lemon juice, nuts and coconut. Cook over high heat, stirring constantly until the fruit mixture comes to a full boil. Add the sugar, stirring constantly, and boil hard for 1 minute. Remove from heat and add the pectin. Skim and stir for 5 minutes. Pour into hot containers and seal at once. Nine 6-ounce glasses.

Sallie P. Satterly, Hitchins, Kentucky

TOMATO-APPLE CONSERVE

2 lemons, thinly sliced	1/2 tsp. salt
5 lb. ripe tomatoes,	2 c. chopped walnuts
6 lge. cooking apples	1 1/2 c. raisins
6 c. sugar	1/2 c. chopped candied ginger

Place the lemon slices in a heavy kettle and add 2 cups water. Bring to a boil and simmer for about 50 minutes or until the rind is soft. Peel, core, and chop the tomatoes and apples, then add with sugar and salt to the lemons. Heat, stirring often, until the sugar dissolves. Cook, stirring and skimming, for 45 minutes. Add the walnuts, raisins and ginger to the cooked mixture. Cook, stirring several times, for about 15 minutes or until the syrup is thick and the fruit is clear. Pour in hot sterilized glasses and seal.

Mrs. Bennett Wood, Bay St. Louis, Mississippi

Apple Chutney (below)

APPLE CHUTNEY

10 c. sliced peeled cooking apples	1 c. sliced dried figs
1 qt. cider vinegar	2 tbsp. salt
2 lb. brown sugar	2 tbsp. ground ginger
1 c. chopped onion	2 tbsp. pickling spices, tied in bag
1 1/2 c. raisins	1 tsp. cayenne pepper

Place the apples in a large kettle and add the vinegar. Add the remaining ingredients and bring to a boil over medium heat, stirring frequently. Reduce the heat and simmer, uncovered, for 2 hours, stirring occasionally. Remove the spice bag. Ladle the mixture immediately into hot sterilized jars to within 1/8 inch of the top. Wipe top and threads of jar with a clean, damp cloth and seal. Invert jar for several seconds; then stand upright to cool. Store jars in a cool, dark dry place. Eight 8-oz. jars.

APPLE PRESERVES

10 lb. apples	8 lb. sugar
Salt	

Peel and slice the apples thin and drop into salted water. Drain and rinse. Layer the apples and sugar in a kettle and stir well. Let stand for 24 hours. Heat to boiling point, then reduce heat and simmer until the syrup thickens as for jelly. Pour into hot sterilized jars and seal.

Mrs. Athel Phillips, North Wilkesboro, North Carolina

APRICOT PRESERVES

2 lb. firm ripe apricots   1/4 c. lemon juice
3 1/4 c. sugar

Wash, scald, pit and peel the apricots. Add the sugar and lemon juice and let stand for 4 to 5 hours. Cook over low heat, stirring until the sugar dissolves. Boil over high heat until the apricots are clear. Pour immediately into hot sterilized jars and seal.

Barbara Dawson, Sarasota, Florida

CANTALOUPE PRESERVES

1 cantaloupe   2 tbsp. lemon juice
3 1/2 c. sugar

Wash the cantaloupe and cut in 8 slices. Remove the rind and seeds, then cut the slices into even pieces. Add the sugar to the cantaloupe pieces and mix well. Let stand overnight in a cool place. Add the lemon juice and bring to a boil. Boil until the cantaloupe is clear. Pour immediately into hot sterilized jars and seal.

Mrs. Joyce Lee, Brookhaven, Mississippi

CATHEDRAL PRESERVES

1 c. currants   2 c. raspberries
5 c. sugar   2 c. pitted sweet cherries
2 c. loganberries

Crush the currants in a saucepan and add 1 cup water. Cook until soft and turn into a jelly bag to drain. Add the sugar to the currant juice and bring to a boil over low heat, stirring until the sugar is dissolved. Boil over high heat for 5 minutes. Add the remaining ingredients and cook over high heat for about 30 minutes, stirring frequently, or just until the liquid sheets from a spoon. Pour immediately into hot sterilized jars and seal.

Mrs. Lucille Hatch, Yuma, Arizona

CRANBERRY PRESERVES

2 2/3 c. sugar   2 qt. cranberries

Combine the sugar and 3 cups water and bring to a boil, stirring until the sugar is dissolved. Add the cranberries and simmer until the skins burst. Pack the berries in hot sterilized jars. Boil the syrup until thick, then pour over the cranberries and seal.

Mrs. Lillian Peoples, Paducah, Kentucky

SPICED CHERRY PRESERVES

6 c. sugar	1/2 tsp. red food coloring
3 1-lb. cans red, tart	1 3-in. cinnamon stick
pitted cherries, drained	1/2 tsp. whole cloves
1/4 c. lemon juice	6 oz. liquid fruit pectin

Combine all ingredients except the fruit pectin in a 4 to 6-quart kettle and mix well. Bring to a rolling boil and boil for 1 minute, stirring constantly. Add pectin all at once and bring to a boil, then remove from heat. Skim off the foam and cool for 5 minutes, skimming and stirring to distribute fruit. Ladle into sterilized jars or glasses. Cover immediately with paraffin. 8 glasses.

Eula Mae Lincecum, Amarillo, Texas

COCONUT PRESERVES

1 coconut	3 c. sugar

Make a hole in the coconut with an ice pick and drain and reserve 1 cup milk. Remove the shell and rind and grate the coconut meat. Combine the coconut milk, 3 cups water and the sugar in a saucepan and bring to a boil. Boil, stirring until the sugar is dissolved, for 5 minutes. Add 4 cups grated coconut to the sugar and boil until clear. Pack the coconut in hot jars, then cover with boiling syrup and seal.

Mrs. Patricia Simpson, Carlsbad, New Mexico

CURRANT PRESERVES

4 qt. stemmed currants	Sugar

Place half the currants in a large kettle and add just enough water to prevent sticking, then simmer for 15 minutes. Mash the currants occasionally. Turn into a jelly bag to strain and measure the juice. Measure 2 cups sugar for each cup juice. Simmer the juice for 10 minutes, skimming frequently. Add the sugar, stirring until dissolved, and bring to a boil, then add the remaining currants. Simmer until tender and pack in hot sterilized jars. Cook the syrup until thick, then pour immediately over the currants and seal.

Mrs. Sarah Tyner, Roswell, New Mexico

LOQUAT PRESERVES

1 lb. loquats	1 1/2 c. sugar

Dip the loquats in boiling water until the skins slip, then peel and remove the seed. Combine the sugar and 1 1/2 cups water and bring to a boil. Cook for 5 minutes, stirring to dissolve the sugar. Add the loquats and cook over high heat until clear and the sugar is thick. Pack immediately into hot jars and seal.

Mrs. Wanda Cannon, Cleveland, Mississippi

GRAPE PRESERVES

2 gal. grapes   Juice of 1/2 lemon
4 c. sugar

Place the grapes in a large pan and cover with water. Cook until grape skins pop. Pour into colander over pan and let juice drip for about 30 minutes. Move colander over another pan and mash pulp and remaining juice into pan. Repeat until 4 cups pulp are collected. Place the pulp, sugar and lemon juice in a kettle or saucepan. Cook, stirring to prevent sticking, for 30 minutes or until thick. Pour into sterilized 1/2-pint or 1-pint jars and seal.

Mrs. Harvey Biddle, Millport, Alabama

FIG PRESERVES

1 c. soda   6 lb. sugar
6 qt. figs

Sprinkle the soda over the figs and cover with 6 quarts boiling water and let stand for 10 minutes. Drain off the soda solution and rinse the figs well in clear cold water. Mix the sugar and 4 quarts water and boil for 10 minutes. Skim and add the figs gradually. Cook rapidly for 2 hours or until the figs are clear and tender. Lift the figs out carefully and place in a shallow pan. Boil the syrup until thick as honey. Cover the figs with the syrup. Let stand overnight. Pack cold figs in sterilized jars and fill jars with syrup. Seal and process in boiling water in a waterbath canner for 10 minutes.

Vera Martin, Baton Rouge, Louisiana

PEACH PRESERVES

1 qt. (heaping) sliced peaches   2 tbsp. lemon juice
4 c. sugar

Mix the peaches and 2 cups sugar and bring to a boil. Cook for 10 minutes, stirring occasionally. Remove from heat and add remaining sugar and lemon juice. Cook over medium-high heat for 10 minutes, stirring constantly with a wooden spoon. Cool, stirring occasionally, then pour into sterilized jars and seal.

Mrs. J. D. Brown, Kingsport, Tennessee

PARTY PEAR PRESERVES

4 c. sugar   1 c. light corn syrup
2 c. water   2 qt. sliced pears

Mix the sugar, water and corn syrup in a large saucepan and bring to a boil. Add the pears and cook until pears are tender and syrup is thick. Pour into sterilized jars and seal.

Mrs. Lewis F. Mitchell, McCool, Mississippi

Strawberry Preserves Deluxe (below)

STRAWBERRY PRESERVES DELUXE

1 1/2 qt. firm ripe strawberries	5 c. sugar 1/3 c. lemon juice

Combine the strawberries and sugar in a kettle and let stand for 3 to 4 hours. Bring to a boil slowly, stirring occasionally, until sugar dissolves. Add the lemon juice and cook rapidly for about 10 to 12 minutes or until strawberries are clear and syrup is thick. Pour into a shallow pan and let stand, uncovered, for 12 to 24 hours in a cool place. Shake pan occasionally to distribute strawberries through syrup. Pack into hot sterilized jars, leaving 1/4-inch head space. Adjust caps. Process half-pints and pints for 20 minutes at 185 degrees in a hot-water bath. 4 half-pints.

STRAWBERRY PRESERVES

1 qt. strawberries 1 tbsp. vinegar	1 qt. sugar

Place the strawberries and vinegar in a kettle and bring to a boil. Boil for 5 minutes. Add sugar and return to a boil. Boil for 5 minutes. Add sugar and return to a boil. Boil for 15 minutes. Let stand for 24 hours, stirring frequently. Ladle into sterilized jars and seal with hot paraffin.

Photograph for this recipe on page 16.

PEAR PRESERVES WITH GELATIN

3 lb. peeled pears
2 tbsp. lemon juice
1 box powdered pectin

1 3-oz. box lemon gelatin
5 1/2 c. sugar

Core and slice the pears. Mix the pears and lemon juice and add the pectin and gelatin. Bring to a full boil over high heat, stirring occasionally. Add the sugar and return to a full rolling boil. Boil for 1 minute, stirring constantly. Remove from heat and skim off foam with a metal spoon. Ladle into sterilized jars, leaving 1/2-inch headspace. Place lids on jars and screw band on tightly. Invert jars until all are sealed. Stand upright and cool. Pears will pick up flavor of the gelatin. Nine 6-ounce jars.

Mrs. Kenneth J. Songy, Kenner, Louisiana

PINEAPPLE PRESERVES

1 fresh pineapple

Sugar

Peel the pineapple and remove the eyes. Slice in half and cut out the core. Cube the flesh or cut in long sticks, as desired. Add 3 cups sugar for each 2 pounds pineapple and let stand overnight. Bring to a boil and cook until the pineapple is clear and the syrup is thick. Pack in hot sterilized jars and seal.

Mrs. June Ingram, El Paso, Texas

PLUM PRESERVES

2 1/2 lb. tart plums

4 c. sugar

Wash the plums thoroughly and remove the pits. Combine the sugar and 1 cup water and add the plums. Bring to a boil over low heat, stirring until the sugar dissolves. Increase the heat and boil for about 15 minutes or almost to the jellying point. Pour immediately into hot jars and seal.

Mrs. Jo Ann Wheeler, Hopkinsville, Kentucky

GEORGIA WATERMELON RIND PRESERVES

4 lb. watermelon rind
Salt
1 tsp. dissolved alum
9 c. sugar

2 lemons, thinly sliced
Gingerroot to taste
Cinnamon to taste
Allspice to taste

Peel the green skin from the rind, then cut in cubes. Soak the watermelon rind in salted water and alum overnight, using 1 1/2 tablespoons salt to each 2 quarts water. Drain. Cover with fresh water and bring to a boil, then drain. Mix the sugar and 8 cups water and add lemons, gingerroot, cinnamon and allspice. Cook until syrupy, then place the rind in boiling syrup. Boil slowly until rind is tender. Pack in hot sterilized jars and seal immediately.

Mrs. Pearl Farris, Savannah, Georgia

CRISP WATERMELON RIND

5 lb. watermelon rind	1 qt. cider vinegar
1 tbsp. salt	4 2-in. cinnamon sticks
8 tsp. alum	2 tsp. whole allspice
9 c. sugar	2 tsp. whole cloves

Cut off and discard the green and red portion from watermelon rind, leaving only the white inner rind. Cut the rind into 1 to 1 1/2-inch pieces, to measure 4 quarts. Place the rind in a large enamel or stainless steel pot. Add water to cover and stir in the salt. Bring to a boil, then reduce heat and simmer for 15 to 20 minutes or until rind can be easily pierced with a fork. Remove from heat and stir in the alum. Cool, then cover and let stand for 24 hours. Pour off the water, then rinse and drain rind well. Add the sugar, vinegar and cinnamon sticks. Tie the allspice and cloves in a cheesecloth bag and add to watermelon rind mixture. Mix well, then bring just to a boil, stirring constantly. Remove from heat and cool, uncovered. Cover and let stand for 24 hours longer. Drain off the syrup into a large saucepan and bring just to a boil. Pour over the rind and cool. Cover and let stand for 24 hours longer. Drain off the syrup and bring just to a boil. Pour over the rind and cool. Cover and let stand for 24 hours longer. Heat the rind in the syrup, but do not boil. Remove and discard the spice bag. Pack the rind and cinnamon in hot, sterilized jars. Heat the syrup to boiling, then fill jars with boiling syrup. Seal immediately. Store for at least 4 weeks or longer before serving. 4 quarts.

Crisp Watermelon Rind (above)

SOUTHERN CINNAMON-PUMPKIN PRESERVES

8 lb. cubed pumpkin meat	1/8 tsp. salt
5 lb. sugar	3/4 tbsp. oil of cinnamon

Place pumpkin in a large enamel or porcelain pot and cover with sugar. Let set overnight or for at least 12 hours. Cook over medium heat, stirring, to the boiling point. Boil until the syrup forms two drops on a metal spoon or candy thermometer reaches heavy syrup point. Add salt and oil of cinnamon. Do not use powdered cinnamon. Remove from heat and stir. Pack into hot jars and seal or cool and taste. Add more cinnamon, if desired, then reheat and pack into jars. May be served with hot buttered biscuits, rolls or toast for breakfast or as an accompaniment to meats. 4-6 pints.

Sarah A. McCreight, Morganton, North Carolina

TOMATO PRESERVES

7 lb. ripe tomatoes	4 lemons, thinly sliced
5 lb. sugar	1/4 c. ginger

Peel the tomatoes and cut into chunks, then add the sugar and lemons. Cook slowly until transparent and slightly thickened and stir in ginger. Cook over low heat for 5 minutes. Pour into hot sterilized jars and seal. 6 pints.

Mildred H. Dodge, Russell, Kentucky

GOLDEN PRESERVES

2 lb. yellow tomatoes	Grated rind of 1 orange
3 c. sugar	Grind rind of 1 lemon
Juice of 2 oranges	2 lemons, thinly sliced

Pour boiling water over the tomatoes and let stand to loosen skins, then plunge in cold water. Peel and place in a bowl in alternating layers with the sugar. Cover and let stand for about 12 hours. Drain the juice and sugar into a large kettle and add the orange juice and the rinds. Boil until the syrup spins a thread. Add the tomatoes and lemon slices, then increase the heat and cook until thick. Pour into hot sterilized jars and seal.

Mrs. Eleanor McCracken, High Point, North Carolina

QUINCE PRESERVES

3 lb. quinces	3 c. sugar

Peel and quarter the quinces and remove the cores. Combine the sugar and 2 quarts water and boil for 5 minutes. Add the quinces and cook, stirring, until clear red and the syrup is thick almost to the jellying point. Pour immediately into hot jars and seal.

Mrs. Joyce Hill, Anderson, South Carolina

BRANDIED FRUIT

Peaches	Strawberries (opt.)
Sugar	Brandy
Grapes	Bananas, sliced in rounds
Plums	

Peel, pit and slice the peaches. Make a layer in an earthenware jar and sprinkle with sugar and let stand for 24 hours. Wash the grapes, then cut in halves or quarters and place in the jar with the peaches. Sprinkle with sugar and let set overnight. Wash the plums and cut in quarters or eighths, then cover with sugar. Let set for 24 hours. Other fruits such as strawberries may be added when seasonal. Remove the fruit from the jar and drain, reserving the syrup. Measure the syrup and add water if desired. Add 1 pint of brandy for every pint of syrup and mix well. Arrange the fruit in a compote and garnish with the bananas. Pour the brandy mixture over the fruit to serve.

Brandied Fruit (above)

pickles and relishes

For many homemakers, preserving foods means first and foremost pickling and preparing relishes. These women know that there is a fine art to transforming cucumbers into crisp, crunchy pickles and that the blending of various foods to make relishes is creativity personified. In this section, *Southern Living* homemakers share with you their prized recipes for pickles and relishes.

Before you try one of these recipes, review the two pages of tips and instructions for preparing pickles and relishes that follow. This up-to-date information will save you time and help insure that your pickles are the crunchiest and your relishes the most savory!

After you've read these instructions, explore the pages of recipes that follow. Why not prepare Christmas Pickles, a tantalizing blend of pickles and cherries that makes a perfect holiday gift? Or turn your talents to preparing Pickled Crab Apples . . . Old-Fashioned Spiced Oranges . . . Pickled Pole Beans . . . Ginger Pickled Beets . . . Cabbage-Celery Relish . . . Sweet Chowchow . . . Easy-to-Make Corn Relish . . . or any of the recipes you'll find in this section.

When you've finished, you'll have shelves full of home-made pickles and relishes ready to serve your family and guests or to give as gifts. And how proud you'll be to know that you preserved them yourself, with time-honored recipes like those in this section.

131

Pickles and relishes are whole, sliced, or chopped fruits or vegetables that are canned in a salt or vinegar solution. Some relishes and most pickles are canned by the water-bath method. Generally enough preservative salt or vinegar is used to prevent the growth of spoilage-causing microorganisms but there is the danger of organisms getting in the jar as it is being filled. For best results in canning pickles and relishes, use good quality ingredients, measure them accurately, and follow specific recipe directions closely.

PRODUCE

Fruits and vegetables — Produce should be fresh, firm, unbruised, and undecayed. Slightly underripe fruits are best for pickling because they maintain natural shape and desirable texture. Cucumbers and green tomatoes should be small-to medium-sized and preferably pickled within 24 hours of harvesting. Use varieties of cucumbers specially grown for pickling.

instructions
FOR PICKLES AND RELISHES

INGREDIENTS

Salt — Use pure refined dairy, pickling, or kosher salt. Don't use free-flowing table salt, which tends to cloud the brine. Pound for pound granulated and flake salts have the same strength, but they do not measure the same. When using a flake salt, increase the measure by one-half.

Vinegar — Cider or white distilled vinegar free of sediment and with 40 to 60 percent grain strength (4 to 6 percent acidity) should be used. Most vinegar marketed has this strength, but read the bottle label to be sure. Don't use vinegar of unknown grain strength.

Spices and herbs — Use fresh spices and herbs. Whole spices should be tied in a piece of cloth loosely enough to allow the pickling liquid to flow through the cloth. Remove the spice bag before packing the food into jars. Don't allow spices to remain in the pickles too long, since they may cause darkening or too strong a flavor.

Water — Use soft water for making the liquid solution. Minerals in hard water tend to interfere with the pickling process. Or, if water is hard, boil it for 15 minutes, let stand for 24 hours, and remove scum that accumulates on the top. When ready to use the water, carefully ladle it so that the sediment in the bottom is not disturbed. Add 1 tablespoon vinegar per gallon of boiled water before using.

Lime — Use calcium hydroxide, sometimes called slaked lime or builders' lime. Lime should be powdered, not lumpy. Do not use quicklime. Slaked lime can be purchased at feed and seed stores, hardware stores, some drugstores, and so on.

EQUIPMENT

Brass, copper, iron, and zinc utensils should not be used, for they tend to cause undesirable color changes. Use enamelware, glass, stainless steel, or stoneware utensils when preparing and canning pickles and relishes. Do not use aluminum or plastic containers when fermenting cucumbers.

PREPARATION

1. Read the recipe. Check the manufacturer's instructions for filling and sealing jars. Assemble equipment and ingredients.

2. If the open-kettle method is to be used, jars must be sterilized. To sterilize, cover jars in pan with hot water and put on stove to heat. Bring water to a boil; boil jars for 10 minutes, new lids, caps, and rings for 5 minutes. If a recipe calls for water-bath processing, wash jars and fittings in soapy water and rinse. They need not be sterilized.

3. Sort produce for size and maturity. Wash thoroughly and drain. Most fruits and vegetables are peeled, and most fruits are also cored or pitted. FOLLOW SPECIFIC RECIPE INSTRUCTIONS FOR PROPER PREP-ARATION OF FRUITS, VEGETABLES, AND LIQUID SOLUTION. Recipes for vegetable pickles may call for long brine curing – 6 to 8 weeks. Follow your recipe closely.

4. Pack pickles that are *not* to be processed when they are boiling hot. Cover with boiling hot liquid to within 1/4 inch of top of jar. Fill and immediately seal one jar at a time. For pickles that are to be processed in a water-bath canner, fill hot jars to within 1/2-inch of the top. Cover with liquid.

5. Remove air bubbles by running a metal spatula scraper or similar uten-sil between the jar and the food. If needed, add more liquid to cover. *Make sure that the produce is covered.* If there is not enough pickling solution to cover fruits or vegetables, add more vinegar.

6. Wipe tops and necks of jars clean. Seal with glass or enamel-lined lids.

7. For pickles that are not to be processed, stand jars upright on cloth or wood surface to cool. Or, process pickles by the water-bath method (see pages 9-10 and pages 34-37) for proper length of time (see pages 180-182).

8. About 12 hours later, test jars for sealing. If a jar has failed to seal, either reheat the food to boiling and repack it in sterilized jars for the open-kettle method; or repack the food and reprocess it the full length of time in a water-bath canner. The food may be refrigerated and used as soon as possible.

9. Store jars in a dark, dry, cool area. Pickles have a better blended and mellower flavor if permitted to stand a few months before consumption.

CHRISTMAS PICKLES

3 c. sugar
1 c. apple vinegar
1/2 lb. candied red cherries

1 qt. dill pickles, sliced
thin

Dissolve the sugar in vinegar in a saucepan and add the cherries and dill pickles. Cook for 1 to 2 minutes, then pack in sterilized jars. Seal the jars.

Dorothy Billings, Fairfax, Virginia

SPICED FRESH CHERRIES

2 lb. firm ripe fresh sweet
cherries
3 c. brown sugar

2 c. cider vinegar
2 tbsp. mixed pickling spice
1/4 tsp. salt

Leave stems attached to cherries and set aside. Combine the sugar, vinegar and 1/2 cup water in a large saucepan. Tie the mixed pickling spice in a cheesecloth bag and add to the sugar mixture, then stir in the salt. Bring to a boil and boil for 2 to 3 minutes. Add the cherries and bring to boiling point. Remove the spice bag. Pack in hot sterilized jars, leaving 1/2-inch space at the top of jars. Seal at once. Do not open for about 6 weeks. 5 half-pint jars.

Photograph for this recipe on page 5.

PICKLED FIGS

5 qt. firm ripe figs
1 c. soda
4 to 5 c. sugar
2 1/2 c. vinegar
1 tsp. salt
1/4 tsp. ground nutmeg

2 tsp. whole cloves
2 tsp. whole allspice
1 med.-sized piece of
gingerroot
3 sticks cinnamon
Green food coloring

Place the figs in a large bowl, then sprinkle with the soda and add 6 quarts boiling water. Let stand for 5 minutes, then thoroughly rinse the figs in cool water and drain. Bring 2 1/2 cups sugar and 2 quarts water to a boil in a saucepan. Add the figs and cook for 30 minutes or until tender. Add remaining sugar, vinegar, salt, nutmeg and whole spices, tied in a piece of thin cloth. Cook until the figs are clear. Let stand in a cool place overnight. Add the coloring, if desired. Pack the figs to within 1/2 inch of the top of fruit jars. Bring the syrup to a boil and pour over the figs. Place the lids on the jars and screw bands tight. Process for 15 minutes in boiling water. 5 or 6 pints.

SPICED KUMQUATS

1 qt. kumquats
3 c. sugar
1 c. vinegar

1 stick cinnamon
1 tbsp. whole cloves
1 tbsp. whole allspice

Wash the kumquats and cut a thin slice across the top. Cover with water and bring to a boil. Cook for 10 minutes, then drain. Combine the sugar, vinegar and 3 cups water in a large saucepan and bring to a boil. Tie the spices in a piece of cloth and drop into the syrup. Cook for 5 minutes. Add the kumquats and cook for 10 minutes, then discard the spice bag. Let the kumquats stand overnight, then, bring to a boil and cook until the syrup is thick. Pack the kumquats into hot sterilized jars and cover with syrup. Place the lids on the jars and screw bands tight. Process for 10 minutes in boiling water.

PICKLED CRAB APPLES

4 lb. ripe crab apples	1/2 tbsp. allspice
4 1/2 c. sugar	1 1 1/2-in. piece of
2 1/2 c. vinegar	gingerroot
2 c. water	2 sticks cinnamon
1 tsp. salt	Red food coloring
1/2 tbsp. whole cloves	

Wash and rinse the crab apples, then drain. Remove the blossom end and prick the crab apples with a large needle. Place the sugar, vinegar, water, salt and spices, tied in a piece of thin cloth, in a wide pan or kettle. Cook, stirring, until the sugar dissolves. Add one layer of crab apples and boil gently for 7 minutes. Replace each layer with another layer until all the crab apples are cooked, then add a few drops of color to the syrup. Pour the syrup over the crab apples, then add the spice bag. Cover and let stand in a cool place for 24 to 48 hours. Pack the crab apples to within 1/2 inch of the top of the fruit jars. Heat the syrup to boiling and pour over the crab apples. Place the lids on the jars and screw bands tight. Process pints and quarts for 20 minutes in boiling water. 4 to 6 pints.

(Clockwise) Spiced Kumquats (page 134); Pickled Figs (page 134); Pickled Crab Apples (above); Pickled Watermelon Rind (page 138). Above: Pickled Peaches (page 136)

EASY PICKLED CRAB APPLES

12 qt. yellow crab apples	12 c. sugar
1 1-oz. stick cinnamon, broken	6 c. cider vinegar
1/2 oz. whole cloves	8 c. water

Wash the crab apples and pack into sterilized quart jars. Divide the stick cinnamon and whole cloves among the jars. Combine the sugar, vinegar and water in a saucepan and bring to a boil. Cover the apples with boiling syrup. Place the lids and rings on the jars and process in a boiling water bath for 18 to 20 minutes or until skins on crab apples begin to break. 12 quarts.

Photograph for this recipe on page 5.

PICKLED GREEN GRAPES

1 c. sugar	3 2-in. sticks cinnamon
1 c. water	1 piece of whole ginger
1/4 c. cider vinegar	3 c. green seedless grapes

Combine the sugar, 1/4 cup water and the vinegar in a saucepan. Add the cinnamon and ginger. Bring to a boil and boil for 3 to 4 minutes. Remove from heat and add the grapes. Return to a boil over high heat and remove from heat immediately. Pack in hot sterilized jars to within 1/2 inch of top. Seal at once. Let stand for at least 1 week before serving. Serve as a relish for poultry or meats. 3 half-pint jars.

Photograph for this recipe on page 5.

OLD-FASHIONED SPICED ORANGES

6 oranges	2 2-in. sticks cinnamon
2 c. sugar	3/4 tsp. whole cloves

Wash the oranges. Cut each orange into 6 wedges and place in a large bowl. Add the sugar, then toss and cover. Let stand for at least 8 to 10 hours or overnight to draw out juice. Drain the oranges, reserving juice. Set the oranges aside for later use. Measure the juice and add enough water to make 3 cups liquid. Place the liquid in a large saucepan with spices. Bring to boiling point and boil for 5 minutes. Add the oranges and return to boiling point. Reduce the heat and simmer, uncovered, for 20 minutes longer or until the skins are slightly transparent. Pack the oranges and spices in hot sterilized jars. Fill jars to within 1/2 inch of top with syrup and seal immediately. 2 quart jars.

Photograph for this recipe on page 130.

PICKLED PEACHES

6 c. sugar	1 tsp. salt
4 c. vinegar	1/2 tsp. ginger
3 sticks cinnamon	1/2 tsp. mace
1 tbsp. whole cloves	8 lb. small firm ripe peaches
1 tbsp. whole allspice	

Combine the sugar and vinegar in a large kettle. Tie the cinnamon, cloves and allspice in a cloth and add to the vinegar mixture. Add the salt, ginger and mace. Bring to a boil and stir until the sugar is dissolved, then simmer for about 30 minutes. Dip the peaches in boiling water until the skins slip easily, then dip in cold water and peel. Add several peaches at a time to the boiling syrup and boil for 4 to 5 minutes. Pack the hot peaches in hot sterilized jars and cover with hot syrup. Place the lids on the jars and screw the bands tight. Process for 20 minutes in boiling water in a waterbath canner.

Photograph for this recipe on page 135.

PICKLED PEACHES WITH BROWN SUGAR

2 tbsp. vinegar	1 tbsp. cloves
Salt	3 sticks cinnamon
24 to 30 sm. firm ripe peaches	3 c. red wine vinegar
1 piece of gingerroot	5 c. light brown sugar
1 tbsp. allspice	

Combine 1 quart water, vinegar and 2 tablespoons salt and set aside. Scald the peaches to loosen the skins, then dip in cold water and peel. Drop into salted vinegar water to prevent darkening. Tie the spices in a piece of thin cloth. Combine 1 teaspoon salt, 2 cups water, wine vinegar and 1/2 of the sugar in a wide pan and stir until well mixed. Add the spice bag and bring to a boil. Add a layer of peaches and boil over low heat for about 5 minutes. Repeat until all the peaches have been heated through, then pour the hot syrup over all the peaches. Cover and let stand overnight in a cool place. Discard the spice bag and pack the peaches to within 1/2 inch of the top of the hot sterilized jars. Add remaining sugar to the syrup and boil until the sugar dissolves. Pour the hot syrup over the peaches and remove air bubbles with a table knife. Add more syrup if needed to cover the peaches. Place the lids on the jars and screw bands tight. Process for 20 minutes in boiling water in a waterbath canner.

Pickled Peaches with Brown Sugar (above)

137

SPICED PEACHES

4 c. sugar	1 tbsp. whole allspice
2 c. cider vinegar	1 tbsp. whole cloves
4 2-in. sticks cinnamon	5 lb. firm ripe peaches

Combine the sugar, vinegar, 1 cup water and cinnamon in a large saucepan. Tie the allspice and cloves in a cheesecloth bag and add, mixing well. Cover and cook over high heat for 5 minutes. Dip the peaches in boiling water for 1 minute and then in cold water. Remove the skins. Simmer the peaches in spiced syrup for 10 to 15 minutes or until peaches are tender. Pierce with a toothpick to test. Transfer the peaches to hot, sterilized jars, packing a stick of cinnamon in each jar. Fill the jars to within 1/2 inch of top with boiling syrup and seal at once. Let stand for 6 to 8 weeks before using. 2 quarts or 4 pints.

Photograph for this recipe on page 130.

PICKLED PEARS

4 lb. Seckel pears	1 c. water
4 c. sugar	1 tbsp. whole cloves
1/2 tsp. salt	1 tbsp. whole allspice
1/2 tsp. ground mace	2 3-in. sticks cinnamon
Light vinegar	

Wash, rinse and drain the pears. Place sugar, salt, mace, 2 cups vinegar, water and whole spices, tied in thin piece of cloth in a kettle. Cover and bring to a boil, then let simmer while preparing pears. Peel the pears and remove the blossom end. Combine 2 tablespoons vinegar and 4 quarts water in a large bowl. Drop each peeled pear in the salt-vinegar water to help prevent darkening. Drain the pears, then drop pears into the hot pickling syrup and let boil slowly for 20 minutes. Pack the hot pears to within 1/2 inch of the tops of the fruit jars and add hot syrup to cover. Place the lids on the jars and screw the bands tight. Process for 20 minutes in boiling water. 3 or 4 pints.

PICKLED WATERMELON RIND

4 qt. watermelon rind	1 tbsp. whole cloves
2 tbsp. salt	1 qt. vinegar
1/4 c. broken stick cinnamon	8 c. sugar

Remove the peel and pink portion from watermelon rind and cut into 2-inch squares. Simmer in salted boiling water to cover until rind is tender, then drain thoroughly. Chill in very cold water for at least 1 hour or overnight and drain. Tie the spices in a bag. Bring the vinegar and sugar to a boil. Add spices and drained watermelon rind. Simmer until rind is clear and transparent, then remove spice bag. Pack the rind into hot sterilized jars. Cover with boiling syrup and seal immediately. 4-5 pints.

Photograph for this recipe on page 135.

LEMON-PEACH PICKLES

6 peaches, peeled and halved	**1 c. sugar**
12 cloves	**2 tbsp. lemon juice**

Place the peaches in a single layer in a shallow baking dish. Stick 2 cloves into each half. Sprinkle with sugar, then drizzle lemon juice over all. Cover. Bake at 350 degrees for about 30 minutes. Turn peaches once. Pack into hot sterilized jars. Bring remaining syrup to a boil, dissolving sugar, then pour over peaches. Seal. Process for 10 minutes in boiling water in a waterbath canner.

Mrs. Edith Shore, East Bend, North Carolina

VEGETABLE PICKLES

4 lb. green gherkins	**3 qt. vinegar**
2 lb. green peas	**5 c. sugar**
2 lb. green beans	**1/2 c. prepared mustard**
2 lb. small young onions	**1/2 c. curry**
2 lb. carrots	**1 c. flour**
2 heads cauliflower	

Prepare the vegetables as for cooking. Cut the carrots in thick slices and separate the cauliflower into flowerets. Combine 3 tablespoons salt to 1 quart water, preparing enough to soak each vegetable separately in salt water. Let the vegetable stand overnight in salt water, then drain. Pour the vinegar in a large kettle and bring to a boil. Add the sugar and the vegetables, a small amount at a time, allowing liquid to remain at the boiling point. Combine the mustard, curry and flour with enough water to make a paste, then add to the boiling mixture. Place the vegetables and liquid in stone jars and cover the tops with waxed paper. Tie the paper securely. Allow the vegetables to stand for about 2 weeks or until fermentation has ceased. Pack the vegetables in hot sterilized jars and cover with the vinegar. Place lids and rings on the jars. Process for 30 minutes in boiling water.

Vegetable Pickles (above)

139

PICKLED ARTICHOKES

5 qt. artichokes	5 whole cloves
Lemon juice	3/4 in. stick cinnamon
1 qt. cider vinegar	1/8 tsp. mace
1 1/2 tsp. whole pickling	1/8 tsp. thyme leaves
spices	1/2 c. sugar

Select small artichokes, if used whole. Clean and rub each with lemon juice, then set aside. Pour the vinegar in a saucepan. Tie the pickling spices, cloves, cinnamon, mace and thyme in a thin cloth bag and add to the vinegar. Let steep for 45 minutes. Add the sugar and bring the mixture to a boil. Reduce the heat and simmer for 20 minutes. Add 1 pint artichokes, a small amount at a time and boil for 1 minute. Pack immediately in hot canning jars. Continue process until all the artichokes are cooked. Bring spiced vinegar to a boil and pour in jars, covering artichokes, leaving 3/4-inch headspace. Adjust lids. Process in a water bath at 212 degrees for 10 minutes. 5 pints.

Ida Lee Murray, Oklahoma City, Oklahoma

PICKLED POLE BEANS

2 lb. pole beans	1 1/2 tsp. mixed pickling
3/4 c. cider vinegar	spice
1/2 c. coarse salt	4 tbsp. dillseed
1 tsp. whole black pepper	2 bay leaves

Remove the tips from the beans. Cook the beans in boiling salted water for 8 minutes. Drain and pack in sterilized quart jars. Combine 2 quarts water, vinegar, coarse salt, black pepper, pickling spice, dillseed and bay leaves in a large, deep saucepan. Bring to a full rolling boil. Pour the vinegar mixture over the beans, covering completely. Seal the jars and let stand for at least 2 days for flavor to penetrate the beans. Use within 2 weeks. 2 quarts.

Photograph for this recipe on page 130.

DILLY BEANS

3 lb. tender whole green beans	1 tsp. red pepper
4 cloves of garlic	4 c. vinegar
4 sprigs of dill	1/4 c. coarse salt

Scald beans and pack into sterilized pint jars. Place 1 clove of garlic, 1 sprig of dill and 1/4 teaspoon red pepper in each jar. Combine 4 cups water, the vinegar and salt in a saucepan and bring to a boil. Pour over the beans and seal. Allow to stand for at least 2 weeks before using.

Eva D. Samples, Procious, West Virginia

GINGER PICKLED BEETS

10 to 15 cooked beets	2 tbsp. prepared horseradish
3 c. vinegar	2 tbsp. sugar

1 tsp. ground mace
1 tsp. ground ginger

1/2 tsp. ground cloves

Leave small beets whole and slice large beets. Place the beets in a hot, sterilized quart jar or 2 pint jars. Combine the vinegar and 1 cup water with remaining ingredients in a saucepan. Bring to boiling point and boil for 2 minutes. Pour over beets to within 1/2 inch of top of jar. Seal the jars and let stand for 24 hours before serving. 1 quart.

Photograph for this recipe on page 130.

RAINBOW PICKLED PEPPERS

1 qt. sweet red peppers
1 qt. green peppers
1 qt. yellow peppers
1 c. salt

1 qt. vinegar
2 tbsp. sugar
1 tbsp. grated horseradish
1 clove of garlic

Wash the peppers and cut in rings, removing the seeds. Place in a large shallow dish and sprinkle with the salt. Pour about 6 cups of water over the peppers and let stand overnight. Drain the peppers, then rinse and drain again. Combine the vinegar with 1 cup water, the sugar, horseradish and garlic. Bring to a boil and simmer for 20 minutes, then discard the garlic. Pack the peppers in alternating colors in hot sterilized jars and cover with the boiling vinegar mixture, then seal. The pickled peppers may be combined with leeks and served with fish, meat or sausage dishes.

Rainbow Pickled Peppers (above)

PICKLED CAULIFLOWER

1 c. plain salt	2 c. sugar
4 qt. cauliflowerets	1/4 c. pickling spice
4 2/3 c. white vinegar	2 c. small onions
1 qt. water	

Add the salt to the cauliflower and let stand for several hours, then rinse and drain. Combine the vinegar, water, sugar and spice and bring to a boil. Add the onions and cauliflowerets and bring to a brisk boil. Pour into sterilized jars and seal.

Mrs. Mary Williams, Moriarty, New Mexico

PICKLED VEGETABLES

2 c. sliced carrots	2 c. sliced celery
2 c. cauliflowerets	6 sweet red peppers,
2 c. sm. cucumbers	coarsely chopped
2 c. sm. pearl onions,	6 pt. white vinegar
peeled	6 pt. water

Place the vegetables in a crock and add enough brine to cover vegetables. Brine should be strong enough to float an egg. Weight vegetables down with a scalded, heavy plate and place fruit jar filled with water on plate. Let set for 2 to 3 weeks or until fermented, removing film from top as fermentation takes place. Drain off brine. Mix the vinegar and water in a saucepan and bring to a boil. Place vegetables in sterilized jars and pour hot vinegar mixture over vegetables to cover. Seal the jars.

Mrs. Bill Dockery, Birmingham, Alabama

GENUINE DILL PICKLES

18 to 20 lb. pickling	4 tbsp. mixed pickling spice
cucumbers	1/4 c. sugar
1 3/4 c. pickling salt	3 bunches dill with seed
1 1/2 c. vinegar	8 or 10 grape leaves

Wash, rinse and drain the cucumbers. Combine the salt, vinegar, spice, sugar and 10 quarts water in a large container. Stir to dissolve the salt. Place 1 or 2 layers of cucumbers in a glass or stoneware crock or jar or a tight, well-scalded, odorless wooden keg. Add some of the dill and 3 or 4 fresh grape leaves, if available. Repeat process until all the cucumbers are in the container. Leave at least 3 inches headspace. Add brine to cover the cucumbers. Use a glass or ceramic plate which will fit inside the container to hold the cucumbers under the brine. Fill a fruit jar with water and use as a weight to hold the plate down. Cover the container with a thin cloth and store in a dry, well-ventilated place. Check the container every day and remove scum which forms on top of the brine. Add brine, if needed, to keep the cucumbers well covered. Let stand for 3 to 4 weeks for the pickles to develop even color and good flavor. A small red pepper, a few sprigs of dill and 1 teaspoon light mustard seed may be added to each quart jar of pickles. Pack the pickles to within 1/2 inch of the tops of the jars. Strain the brine and boil for 5 minutes, then pour over the pickles to about 1/4 inch from the tops of the jars. Wipe off the top or threads of the jars. Place the lids on the jars and screw bands tight. Process for 15 minutes in boiling water.

FRESH-PACK DILL PICKLE

7 qt. 3 to 5-in. cucumbers
1 1/2 c. pickling salt
6 c. vinegar
3/4 c. salt
1/4 c. sugar

2 tbsp. whole mixed pickling
    spices
Whole mustard seed
Dillseed

Wash the cucumbers thoroughly and drain. Combine pickling salt and 2 gallons water for brine. Cover the cucumbers with the brine. Let stand overnight and drain. Combine the vinegar, salt, sugar, 9 cups water and mixed pickling spices, tied in a clean thin cloth in a large kettle and bring to a boil. Let stand and pack the cucumbers into hot sterilized quart jars. Add 2 teaspoons mustard seed and 2 tablespoons dillseed to each jar. Cover with boiling spiced liquid to within about 1/4 inch of the tops of the jars. Wipe off anything spilled on tops or threads of jars. Place the lids on the jars and screw the bands tight Process in boiling water for 20 minutes in a waterbath canner.

Genuine Dill Pickles (page 142)

ICICLE PICKLES

3 1/2 lb. medium-sized
  cucumbers
1 qt. cider vinegar
1/2 c. sugar

1/2 c. salt
1 tbsp. mustard seed
1 tbsp. celery seed

Wash the cucumbers but do not peel. Cut into lengthwise quarters or eighths and soak in ice water for 5 hours. Add ice as necessary to keep the water cold. Drain and pack in hot sterilized jars. Combine the vinegar, sugar, salt, mustard and celery seed in a saucepan. Bring to boiling point and boil for 1 minute. Pour over the cucumbers to within 1/2 inch of the tops of jars and seal at once. Let stand for 4 to 6 weeks before using. 5 pints.

Photograph for this recipe on page 130.

MIXED PICKLES

10 med. cucumbers, cut in
  2-in. strips
Salt
6 lge. carrots, cut in
  2-in. strips
4 red peppers, cut in strips
4 green peppers, cut in strips

4 yellow peppers, cut in
  strips
6 c. sugar
4 c. vinegar
3 tbsp. celery seed
1 tsp. turmeric

Soak cucumbers overnight in heavily salted water; drain. Cook carrots for 5 minutes in small amount of salted water; drain. Combine cucumbers, carrots and peppers; add sugar, vinegar, celery seed, turmeric and 1 teaspoon salt. Bring to a boil. Pour into sterilized 1-pint jars; seal.

Mrs. Fred Riggleman, Dorcas, West Virginia

MUSTARD PICKLES

1 head cauliflower
1 qt. small green tomatoes
3 green peppers
1 qt. pickling onions
24 1-in. cucumbers
1 c. salt

2 c. (or more) sugar
1 1/2 c. flour
1/2 c. dry mustard
1 tbsp. turmeric
7 c. cider vinegar
7 c. water

Cut the vegetables into uniform pieces and cover with salt and 4 cups water. Let stand overnight, then drain. Cover with boiling water and let stand for 15 minutes. Combine remaining ingredients and cook until thick. Add the vegetables. Cook until just tender over low heat. Pack in sterilized jars and seal. One ripe pepper may be substituted for 1 green pepper.

Mrs. H. L. Grant, Roy, New Mexico

GREEN TOMATO PICKLES

7 lb. green tomatoes, sliced	1 tsp. ginger
1 c. slaked lime	1 tsp. cloves
5 lb. sugar	1 tsp. allspice
3 pt. vinegar	

Soak the tomatoes in 2 gallons water with lime for 24 hours. Drain and soak in clear water. Change water every hour, all during the day. Cover with clear water and soak overnight. Drain and soak again if necessary to be sure all the lime is removed. Combine the sugar, vinegar and spices, tied in a small cloth bag. Cook the sugar mixture to syrup consistency and pour over the drained tomatoes. Let stand for 24 hours. Move spice bag around occasionally so all tomatoes are seasoned. Boil the mixture for 1 hour. Remove spice bag, then fill sterilized jars and seal while hot. 6 quarts.

Photograph for this recipe on page 130.

BREAD AND BUTTER PICKLES

30 cucumbers	2 tsp. ground ginger
10 med. onions	4 c. sugar
4 tbsp. salt	1 tsp. turmeric
5 c. vinegar	2 tsp. white mustard seed
2 tsp. celery seed	

Slice the cucumbers and onions and sprinkle with salt. Let stand for 1 hour. Drain in a cheesecloth bag. Combine remaining ingredients in a large kettle and bring to a boil. Add the cucumbers and onions and bring to a boiling point. Simmer for 10 minutes, then pour in sterilized jars. Place caps on jars. Process for 10 minutes at 180 degrees in a waterbath canner.

Mrs. Virgil M. Windham, Burlington, North Carolina

DILL PICKLES

25 cucumbers, 4 in. long	Grape leaves
1/8 tsp. alum	Heads of dill
1 qt. vinegar	Hot red peppers
1 c. pickling salt	Cloves of garlic
3 qt. water	

Wash and split the cucumbers. Cover with cold water, then add alum and let stand overnight. Drain and pack pickles into jars. Make a brine by combining the vinegar, salt and water in a saucepan. Bring to a boil and pour over the pickles. Add 2 grape leaves, 2 heads of dill, 1 pepper and 1 clove of garlic to each jar. Process for 15 minutes in boiling water in a waterbath canner.

Mrs. C. F. Malm, Paducah, Kentucky

SLAKED LIME CUCUMBER PICKLE

7 lb. cucumbers, sliced	5 lb. sugar
2 c. powdered slaked lime	1 tbsp. salt
2 qt. apple vinegar	1 pkg. pickling spice

Cover the cucumbers with the lime and 2 gallons water. Let soak for 24 hours, then drain. Cover with fresh water and soak for 4 hours and drain. Repeat freshwater soaking 4 times. Combine all the remaining ingredients and bring to a boil. Pour the hot vinegar mixture over well-drained cucumbers and let stand overnight. Remove the cucumbers from liquid, reserving liquid. Bring the reserved liquid to boil, then add cucumbers and boil for 2 or 3 minutes. Pack the cucumbers in jars, then cover with hot liquid and seal.

Photograph for this recipe on page 130.

SWEET STICKLES

7 lb. cucumber sticks	Few drops of green food
1 c. slaked lime	coloring
1 1/2 qt. white vinegar	1 1/2 tbsp. celery seed
7 1/2 c. sugar	1 1/2 tbsp. salt

Peel the cucumbers and cut lengthwise, then scoop out the seeds with a spoon. Slice into strips the size of a finger and cut into desired lengths. Mix the lime and 1 gallon water and pour over the cucumbers. Let soak overnight, then wash well until water is clear. Soak in clear water for 3 to 4 hours and drain. Combine the vinegar, sugar, food coloring, celery seed and salt and bring to a boil. Pour over the cucumbers and let stand overnight. Simmer for 30 minutes or until the cucumbers are clear. Lift pickles from bottom of the kettle with a spoon to heat evenly. Pack into jars and seal. 10 pints.

Rose Shular, Columbia, South Carolina

ARTICHOKE RELISH

1 peck artichokes	2 qt. scalded apple cider
2 bunches of celery	vinegar
3 lb. white onions	5 c. sugar
1 cauliflower	1 c. (or more) flour
5 red peppers	1/4 lb. dry mustard
Salt	3 tbsp. turmeric

Brush or scrape the artichokes thoroughly clean. Cut all the vegetables into small pieces and add 1 cup salt. Soak overnight in a cool place. Squeeze the juice from the vegetables and combine with the vinegar, sugar, remaining salt, flour, mustard and turmeric. Heat to boiling point, but do not boil. Remove from heat. Pack in sterilized jars and seal. 10-12 pints.

Mrs. H. R. Rainville, Spartanburg, South Carolina

APPLE RELISH

12 med. onions	7 red sweet peppers
12 med. cooking apples	7 green sweet peppers

3 c. vinegar	Salt to taste
3 c. sugar	

Grind the onions, apples and peppers in a food chopper. Add the vinegar, sugar and salt and cook until tender. Pack in sterilized jars and seal. 6 or 7 pints.

Photograph for this recipe on page 18.

APPLE CHOWCHOW RELISH

1 gal. quartered green tomatoes	2 red sweet peppers, seeded
1 gal. quartered Washington State apples	2 c. sugar
	1 tsp. allspice
1 bunch celery	1 tsp. cinnamon
1 qt. quartered onions	1 tsp. cloves
2 green sweet peppers, seeded	1 qt. cider vinegar
	Salt to taste

Grind the tomatoes and drain. Grind the apples, celery, onions and seeded peppers. Combine the ground ingredients in kettle, then stir in the sugar and spices, mixing well. Add the vinegar, then bring to a boil. Simmer, stirring occasionally, until tender. Season with salt. Pour into hot sterilized jars and seal.

Apple Chowchow Relish (above), Apple-Pineapple Conserve (page 112)

BEAN RELISH

1/2 c. salt	2 c. diced carrots
2 c. chopped green tomatoes	1 can lima beans
2 c. chopped green or red	1 can red kidney beans
peppers	1 can wax beans
2 c. peeled diced cucumbers	3 c. sugar
2 c. chopped onions	3/4 qt. vinegar
2 c. chopped celery	1 tbsp. dry mustard

Make a brine with the salt and 2 quarts water, then add the tomatoes, peppers, cucumbers and onions and soak overnight. Drain. Add the celery, carrots and water to cover and boil for 30 minutes. Drain. Add remaining ingredients and bring to a boil. Pack immediately into hot sterilized jars and seal. 10 pints.

Sara Lu Greeley, Prescott, Arizona

BEET RELISH

3 c. drained and finely chopped	1/4 tsp. cinnamon
beets	1/4 tsp. allspice
1 c. vinegar	1/4 tsp. cloves
6 1/2 c. sugar	1 bottle liquid fruit pectin
2 tsp. prepared horseradish	

Place the beets in a large saucepan and add the vinegar, sugar, horseradish and spices. Mix well. Bring to a rolling boil over high heat and boil for 1 minute, stirring constantly. Remove from heat and stir in liquid pectin at once. Skim. Pour into hot sterilized jars and seal. 4 pints.

Photograph for this recipe on page 32.

CABBAGE-CELERY RELISH

4 lb. shredded cabbage	3 tbsp. dry mustard
1 c. chopped celery	1 tbsp. cornstarch
2 c. chopped onions	1 tbsp. powdered celery seed
1/2 c. salt	1 tbsp. curry powder
2 c. sugar	4 c. cider vinegar

Combine the vegetables and salt in a large bowl. Combine the dry ingredients with enough vinegar to make a smooth paste. Pour the remaining vinegar in a large kettle and bring to a boil. Stir in the paste and cook, stirring constantly, until the sauce is smooth. Add the cabbage mixture and bring again to a boil. Simmer for 10 minutes, then pack in hot sterilized jars and seal.

Mrs. Eunice Gilbert, Jonesboro, Arkansas

SWEET CHOWCHOW

2 gal. chopped cabbage	1/4 c. chopped hot green
1 gal. chopped green tomatoes	peppers
1 qt. chopped onions	1 1/2 lb. sugar

1 tbsp. dry mustard
1 tbsp. ginger
2 tbsp. salt

3 tbsp. cinnamon
3 qt. vinegar

Combine all ingredients in a large kettle and boil until the cabbage is tender. Pour into sterilized jars and seal. 12 pints.

Clara Mae Chatham, Jackson, Mississippi

MEXICAN CORN RELISH

6 ears of fresh corn
2 c. coarsely chopped onion
1 c. coarsely chopped green
　pepper
2 c. coarsely chopped celery
2 c. cider vinegar

1 1/3 c. sugar
1 tsp. powdered mustard
1 tsp. ground turmeric
1 tbsp. salt
1/4 tsp. crushed red pepper
1 c. chopped pimento

Husk and remove the silk from the corn, then cut the kernels from cobs, but do not scrape. Combine small amounts of the onion, green pepper and celery at a time in blender container. Cover and run at high speed until finely chopped. Combine the vinegar, sugar, spices and salt in a heavy kettle, then add the red pepper, pimento, corn and chopped vegetables. Simmer, uncovered, for 20 to 25 minutes, stirring occasionally. Bring to a boil and boil for 5 minutes. Pour into hot sterilized pint jars and seal.

Vegetable Medley (page 154); Mexican Corn Relish (above);
Fresh Pineapple Relish (page 151)

149

Crisp Cucumber Rings (below), Carrot-Pepper Relish (below)

CRISP CUCUMBER RINGS

9 long slender cucumbers	1 1/2 c. sugar
5 med. onions	2 tsp. mustard seed
1/2 c. salt	2 tsp. celery seed
2 c. vinegar	1/2 tsp. hot sauce

Wash and dry the cucumbers, then slice without paring. Peel and slice the onions; add to cucumbers. Combine the salt with 2 cups water and pour over vegetables. Let stand for 3 hours, than drain and discard liquid. Combine the vinegar, sugar and spices in a kettle and stir over medium heat until sugar is dissolved. Add the cucumbers and onions and boil for 5 minutes. Add the hot sauce and pack at once into hot sterilized jars, covering completely with liquid. Seal. 5 pints.

CARROT-PEPPER RELISH

8 med. carrots	2 c. sugar
8 med. onions	2 c. cider vinegar
4 lge. green peppers	1/2 tsp. hot sauce
3 tbsp. salt	

Scrape the carrots, peel the onions and seed the peppers. Slice the vegetables and grind in food chopper, using medium blade. Combine the salt, sugar and vinegar in a kettle; bring to a boil. Add the vegetables and boil for 5 minutes. Add the hot sauce and pack at once into hot sterilized pint or half pint jars. The liquid should cover the vegetables completely. Seal. 4 pints.

FRESH CORN RELISH

9 ears of fresh corn
2 c. finely ground cabbage
1 c. sweet pepper flakes
3/4 c. onion flakes
1 c. sugar
2 1/2 tbsp. salt
2 tsp. crushed red pepper

2 tsp. celery seed
2 tsp. turmeric
1 tsp. mustard seed
1/8 tsp. ground black pepper
2 c. cider vinegar
1/2 c. chopped pimento

Remove the husks and silk from corn. Cut the kernels from the ears. There should be about 9 cups. Place the corn and cabbage in a 5-quart saucepan or preserving kettle with pepper and onion flakes, sugar, salt, spices, vinegar and 1 3/4 cups water. Bring to boiling point, uncovered, and cook for 20 minutes or until relish has thickened. Stir in pimento. Ladle into hot sterilized jars to within 1/2 inch of the top of jars. Seal immediately. Let stand at least 6 weeks before serving. Serve with meat, fish or poultry. 5 pints.

Photograph for this recipe on page 130.

PEAR RELISH

2 gal. pears
1 doz. sweet peppers
1 doz. red hot peppers
1 doz. med. onions
2 c. vinegar

2 c. prepared mustard
3 c. sugar
1 tbsp. salt
2 tsp. celery seed

Peel, quarter and core the pears. Force the pears, peppers and onions through a food chopper. Combine all the ingredients in a large kettle and cook for 25 minutes, stirring occasionally. Fill the jars and seal. 16-18 pints.

Mrs. Aussie A. Miller, Newton, Texas

FRESH PINEAPPLE RELISH

4 tsp. whole cloves
2 tsp. whole allspice
2 1/2 c. sugar
2 1/2 c. cider vinegar

12 c. fresh pineapple chunks
2 7-oz. jars pimento,
   chopped
2 tsp. salt

Tie the cloves and allspice in a cheesecloth bag. Combine the sugar and vinegar in a heavy kettle, then bring to a boil. Boil for 10 minutes, then remove the spice bag. Place small amounts of pineapple into a blender container at a time, then cover and run at low speed. Empty into the kettle, then add the pimento and salt. Bring to a rapid boil, then reduce the heat and cook, uncovered, for 15 minutes, stirring occasionally. Pour into hot sterilized 1/2-pint jars and seal. Serve with pork or ham. 4 pints.

Photograph for this recipe on page 149.

FRESH GARDEN RELISH

2 med. cabbages	2 pt. vinegar
8 lge. carrots	6 c. sugar
12 lge. onions	1 tsp. celery seed
8 green or red peppers	1 tsp. mustard seed
1 c. salt	

Grind the cabbages, carrots, onions and peppers in a food chopper, then add the salt and let stand for 2 hours. Place in a colander and drain. Wash if mixture is too salty. Add the vinegar, sugar, celery seed and mustard seed and stir well. Pour into sterilized jars and seal. 6 pints.

Mrs. Inez P. Curvin, Alexander City, Alabama

PEPPER RELISH

1 doz. sweet green peppers	1 qt. vinegar
1 doz. sweet red peppers	2 tbsp. turmeric
9 hot red peppers	1 tbsp. mixed pickling spices
1 doz. medium onions	3 tbsp. dry mustard
1 doz. apples	2 tbsp. celery seed
1 lb. sugar	

Grind the peppers, onions and apples and drain. Combine all the ingredients in a large kettle and cook over medium heat for 30 minutes. Pour into hot sterilized jars and seal.

Mrs. W. B. Jolly, Taylorsville, Georgia

GRANDMA'S SWEET PEPPER RELISH

1 lge. head cabbage, ground	1 tbsp. celery seed
3 lge. onions, ground	1 tbsp. mustard seed
8 peppers, ground	5 c. sugar
1/2 c. salt	1 qt. vinegar

Combine the cabbage, onions and peppers and cover with water and salt. Let stand for 2 hours. Drain thoroughly, then add celery seed, mustard seed, sugar and vinegar. Let stand for 3 days in a cool place, stirring occasionally. Pack in jars and seal. 5-6 pints.

Mrs. Constance Ackerson, Belle Rose, Louisiana

CHOPPED PICKLE RELISH

12 lge. cucumbers	5 c. sugar
8 green peppers	5 c. vinegar
10 med. onions	3 tbsp. celery seed
4 tbsp. salt	6 tbsp. mustard seed

Slice the cucumbers lengthwise and remove the seeds. Grind the cucumbers, peppers and onions with the coarse blade of the grinder and add salt. Let stand overnight. Drain. Combine remaining ingredients and pour over the vegetable mixture. Bring to a boil and simmer for 20 minutes. Pack in hot jars and seal.

Mrs. Revia C. Munch, Branford, Florida

EASY-TO-MAKE CORN RELISH

6 c. fresh cut corn	1 tsp. crushed red pepper
1 lge. white onion, coarsely chopped	1 1/2 tsp. mixed dried herbs
1 c. chopped celery	2 tsp. salt
1 med. green pepper, coarsely chopped	3 c. white vinegar
	1 1/2 tbsp. ground mustard
1 med. red sweet pepper, coarsely chopped	1/2 tsp. Dijon mustard (opt.)
	2 tbsp. flour
2 cloves of garlic, minced	2 tbsp. corn oil
3/4 c. sugar	1/4 c. water
2 tsp. celery seed	Ascorbic acid (opt.)

Combine all the ingredients except the mustards, flour, oil and water in a preserving kettle. Boil for 5 minutes over moderate heat. Blend the mustards, flour, oil and water together in a small saucepan and cook, stirring constantly, until smooth and thick, then stir into the relish. Cook for 5 minutes, stirring to prevent sticking. Relish should be quite moist but not soupy. Add a small amount of boiling water if too dry. Cook longer if too moist. Pour hot relish into hot sterilized jars, leaving 1/4-inch head space. Run knife gently down side of jar for air to escape. Sprinkle about 1/2 teaspoon ascorbic acid mixture over top of relish, then quickly wipe top of jar and seal. Process pints and half pints for 15 minutes in boiling water bath canner.

Easy-to-Make Corn Relish (above)

Fresh Green Pepper-Cauliflower Relish (below)

FRESH GREEN PEPPER-CAULIFLOWER RELISH

2 med. heads cauliflower	1 tsp. ground turmeric
3 lge. green peppers	2 tsp. mustard seed
16 sm. white onions, peeled	3 tbsp. mixed pickling spice
2 tbsp. salt	1 1/2 c. white vinegar
1 1/4 c. sugar	1 1/2 c. water

Remove the leaves from the cauliflower, then wash and separate into flowerets. Cut the green peppers into thin strips and combine with cauliflower and onions. Sprinkle the vegetables with the salt, then cover and let stand overnight. Drain and rinse in cold water. Combine the sugar, turmeric, mustard seed and pickling spice in a large pot, then stir in the vinegar and water. Bring to a boil and boil for 5 minutes. Add the vegetables and boil gently for 10 minutes, stirring occasionally. Pack in hot sterilized jars. Seal at once. Approximately 4 pints.

VEGETABLE MEDLEY

2 qt. chopped cabbage	2 c. (packed) light brown
1 qt. chopped cucumber	sugar
2 c. chopped green pepper	1/4 c. salt
2 ripe peeled tomatoes,	1 tsp. ground turmeric
quartered	1/2 tsp. ground cloves
2 c. chopped red onion	1/2 tsp. ground allspice
2 7-oz. jars pimento,	1 tsp. dry mustard
chopped	1 tsp. celery seed
1 1/3 c. cider vinegar	

Place the first 5 ingredients in small amounts in blender container. Cover and run at high speed until finely chopped. Empty into a heavy kettle. Add the remaining ingredients, and bring to a rapid boil. Reduce the heat and simmer, uncovered, for 20 to 25 minutes, stirring occasionally. Pour into hot sterilized 1/2-pint canning jars and seal. 5 pints.

Photograph for this recipe on 149.

TOMATO RELISH

12 onions, diced	1 qt. vinegar
2 bunches celery, diced	6 c. sugar
2 green peppers, diced	1 tbsp. cinnamon
1 red pepper, diced	1 tbsp. cloves
1 peck ripe tomatoes, diced	1 tbsp. ginger
1 c. salt	1 tsp. allspice

Combine the vegetables in a large container and add the salt. Let stand overnight and drain. Combine the vinegar, sugar and spices and add to the vegetable mixture. Bring to a boil, then pack in hot sterilized jars and seal.

PEACH CHUTNEY

2 lb. peaches	2 c. vinegar
1 lb. tart apples	4 c. sugar
1 c. chopped celery	2 tsp. salt
2 sweet red peppers, chopped	1 c. seedless raisins

Peel, pit and chop the peaches. Peel, core and chop the apples. Place the celery in a small amount of water in a saucepan and cook until almost tender, then drain. Combine all the ingredients except the raisins and boil over high heat until slightly thickened. Steam the raisins in a small amount of water for about 20 minutes and add to the peach mixture. Pour into hot sterilized jars and seal.

Mrs. Doris Hall, Charleston, South Carolina

RHUBARB CHUTNEY

4 lb. rhubarb	1 tbsp. salt
1 lb. apples	2 tsp. cinnamon
1 lb. seedless raisins	1 tbsp. ginger
1 c. dark corn syrup	1 1/2 tbsp. crushed mustard
2 c. vinegar	seed
1 c. sugar	

Peel the rhubarb and cut the stalk into 1/2-inch pieces. Peel and core the apples, then grind with the raisins in a food chopper. Combine all the ingredients in a large kettle and bring to a boil, stirring until the sugar is dissolved. Reduce the heat and simmer, stirring frequently, for about 25 minutes or until thick. Pack in hot sterilized jars and seal.

Mrs. Jennifer Park, Greenwood, Mississippi

Freezing Fresh Strawberries (page 164)

frozen foods

Years ago, no one thought of freezing foods. In the warm and humid Southland, it was a struggle just to keep foods cool. Every home had its "icebox," a wooden box containing a block of ice. Into this box went the most perishable foods, with a fervent hope that they would keep until they were ready to be served. No one imagined it would ever be possible to *freeze* foods! Today, with modern methods of refrigeration and freezing, iceboxes are a thing of the past. Modern southern homemakers use home freezers to store foods. In this section, you'll find a collection of their recipes for freezing every imaginable kind of food quickly and easily.

Preceding the recipes are four pages of instructions on freezing foods: how to prepare foods for freezing; the proper way to wrap; tips about what foods freeze well and those that don't; and other information to make your freezing of foods easy and successful.

The recipes themselves tell you how to prepare and freeze fruits and jams . . . baked goods and pie fillings . . . many varieties of fish and shellfish . . . mincemeat . . . meats, cooked and uncooked . . . poultry and game birds . . . and vegetables.

For good home economy, use your freezer to store some of the dishes prepared with these recipes. With the recipes and your freezer, you can cut important dollars from your food budget!

157

Freezing, probably the most modern method of food preservation available, is the process of preserving foods at temperatures below 32 degrees. There are two basic units used for freezing foods, the refrigerator freezer compartment and the home freezer. *Refrigerator freezer compartments* are units attached to the top, bottom, or side of refrigerators. The temperatures in these units are below 32 degrees but seldom reach zero degree or lower. For this reason, it is recommended that foods be frozen in these compartments only for short periods of time. As a general rule, foods frozen in refrigerator freezer compartments should be used within a few days. *Home freezers* are upright or chest units that maintain temperatures at zero degree or lower. They are recommended for freezing large quantities of food over long periods of time.

INSTRUCTIONS FOR

freezing foods

Also available are *public freezer lockers,* large storage facilities in which an individual rents space. These lockers can be used as you would a home freezer.

FREEZER PACKAGING

One key to successful freezing of foods is to choose the proper packaging materials. Freezer containers and wrapping paper should be moistureproof and vaporproof. Most aluminum foils, household plastic wrap, and waxed paper are not suitable for freezer wrapping. For best results, food packaged in one of these materials needs an overwrap of freezer paper.

Freezer containers include collapsible square or rectangular boxes used with plastic bags, rigid plastic containers, canning jars, and heavily waxed containers. The *boxes used with plastic bags* may, with care be used several times, but a new plastic bag should be used each time. *Rigid plastic containers* may be used for many years. Each time they are used, they should be carefully checked for cracking or tiny holes and should be washed in warm, soapy water. *Home canning jars* can be used to freeze most foods except those frozen in liquid. Liquid expands when frozen and may cause the glass jar to crack or break. When using a home canning jar, don't fill it above the shoulder or there won't be sufficient head space for the food to expand. *Waxed containers* are less suitable for freezing than are the other three mentioned above. They are difficult to seal, and, moreover, the wax may flake off when the container is moved around in the freezer.

If you are packaging foods for freezing by wrapping them in freezer paper, consult the illustrated instructions on page 161 for step-by-step directions to follow.

FREEZING FOODS

In choosing foods for your freezer, remember to pick first quality, fresh foods. *Fruits* should be ready for eating when you freeze them; discard underripe, overripe, or moldy pieces before freezing. *Vegetables* should be young, tender, and as fresh as possible. *Meat* should have a covering of fat to protect it from drying out; *poultry* should be plump and young; *fish and shellfish* should be freshly caught or have been kept on crushed ice until ready for freezing.

To prepare fruit for freezing, pack dry without sugar, with sugar, with a sugar syrup, or with a sugar substitute. In packing *fruit with sugar,* each piece of fruit should be coated. To prevent the fruit from darkening, add one half to three quarters a teaspoon ascorbic acid (available in drug stores) to each two cups sugar. *Packing fruit in syrup* is recommended to help the fruit hold its shape. Most of the recipes in the pages that follow have the proportions of sugar to water recommended by the women who developed them. But if you want to freeze a fruit and can't find a recipe to go by, try using a 40 percent syrup: that is, one that uses three cups of sugar to four cups of water. This syrup is suitable for most fruits. To keep fruit from coming to the top of any syrup you use, crumple paper on the top of the packed syrup and fruit before sealing the container. If someone in your family is on a special diet, your family physician will recommend the use of a *sugar substitute* in freezing fruit.

To prepare vegetables for freezing, wash thoroughly to remove any dirt, brushing the vegetable if necessary. All vegetables except sweet or bell peppers need to be blanched before freezing. Blanching is done in boiling water, usually in the proportion of one gallon vigorously boiling water to one pound (1 pint) prepared vegetables. Water should be continuously boiling for the entire time specified in the recipe for the vegetables to be blanched. Cool the vegetables in cold running water or in water containing ice. Most vegetables should be drained before they are packed for freezing. Snap beans, peas, and lima beans sometimes have cold water added before the container is sealed, but most other vegetables are packed for freezing without liquid.

To freeze meat or poultry, wrap the food in serving size packages so that you will not thaw more than you need for one meal. If the bones are left in the food, cushion them with crushed paper to prevent their piercing the wrapping paper or container. When freezing poultry that has been stuffed, remove the stuffing and package meat and stuffing separately.

FREEZING COMBINATION DISHES

When freezing a casserole-type dish, a combination of several foods with or without a sauce, there are some precautions to take. Certain foods that normally freeze well present a problem when frozen in combination with other, less easily frozen foods. Some hints to help you follow: *Cheese* as a topping does not freeze well and should be added to a dish only after it is thawed. *Hard-cooked egg whites* should be finely diced or sieved before freezing. They become tough when frozen unless they are in small particles. *Fats* become rancid after two months' freezing time has elapsed. *Mayonnaise* sometimes separates during freezing. Its original consistency can be restored by stirring during thawing. *Meats* that have been frozen uncooked can be thawed, cooked, and refrozen without affecting their flavor. But very small pieces of cooked or uncooked meat dry out when frozen unless they are protected by a sauce or gravy. Sometimes *noodles, spaghetti, and macaroni* that have been cooked get mushy when frozen and thawed. Some varieties of *potatoes* don't freeze well: they break down when thawed and become mushy. Add them to a dish only after thawing. *Sauces* with cheese or milk in their ingredients curdle if they are frozen and reheated; thickened sauces tend to become even thicker. Always avoid freezing egg-based sauces. *Seasonings* may undergo considerable changes during freezing. For example, parsley and chives become soggy; onion and salt become diminished in flavor as do most herbs; garlic and clove become unpleasantly strong; and curry develops a musty flavor. As a general rule, do not include any seasonings in foods or dishes being frozen. Add them after the thawing process is complete.

TIPS FOR SUCCESSFUL FREEZING

Changes in frozen foods that alter the taste, texture, or color of these foods come about because of the chemical action of certain enzymes in food; freezer burn; ice formation during storing; the chemical action of bacteria or mold; and unfavorable storing conditions. Many foods contain *enzymes* that can cause changes in the food. Some of these enzymes make vegetables lose color and flavor. To prevent this loss, blanch all vegetables except peppers and chill them before freezing. *Freezer burn* is the name given to a dry, tough surface that sometimes forms on frozen foods. You can prevent its formation by using moistureproof and vaporproof freezer materials and making sure all air is out of the package before sealing it tightly. Like freezer burn, *ice formations* occur when the food being frozen is improperly packaged. It may also occur when the food is frozen too slowly. To prevent slow freezing, pack only two to three pounds of unfrozen food per cubic foot of freezer space at one time. The *chemical action of bacteria* and mold can be prevented by preparing foods for freezing quickly and using clean equipment. Chill fruits and vegetables to kill bacteria and mold before freezing. *Unfavorable storing conditions* include freezing food for too long a period of time. Most properly packaged, uncooked foods keep in a home freezer for six months to a year. Label all frozen foods with the date they were placed in the freezer so that foods stored longest are used first.

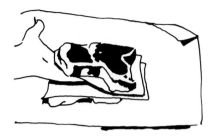

Place the food to be frozen in the middle of a large sheet of moisture-proof, vaporproof freezer paper. If freezing more than one item, place two layers of paper between each item to facilitate thawing.

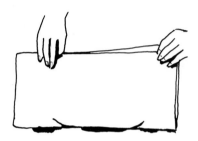

Bring the two sides of the freezer paper together at the top, matching edges.

Fold both sides over about one-half an inch.

Fold over and over again until the edge is resting snugly against the package. Press the flap tightly against the rest of the package.

Turn package over and fold both ends, forcing air out of both sides.

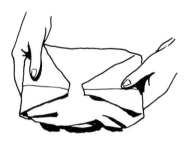

Fold ends under the package, making certain that most of the air is gone from the interior of the package.

Using freezer tape, tape the package closed. Seal all edges completely.

NAME OF FOOD
DATE PACKAGED

Label food and place in freezer.

FROZEN APPLES

2 tbsp. salt   1 qt. sliced peeled apples
1/2 gal. water

Dissolve the salt in the water. Slice the apples into salted water and drain well. Place in plastic bags or freezer containers and seal. Store in freezer.

Mrs. L. H. Roberts, Sweetwater, Oklahoma

FROZEN CINNAMON APPLES

1 c. sugar   1/2 c. red cinnamon candies
1 c. water   8 to 12 med. apples

Combine the sugar, water and candies in a saucepan and cook over medium heat until the candies are dissolved, stirring frequently. Simmer for 5 minutes. Peel the apples and cut in halves. Remove the cores. Cook the apples, several pieces at a time, in the syrup until just tender. Do not overcook and do not crowd apples in syrup. Cool, then place in freezer containers and seal. Freeze.

Mrs. Ann Cochran, Rock Hill, South Carolina

FROZEN BLACKBERRIES

4 qt. blackberries   2 c. sugar

Wash the blackberries carefully in iced water, then drain in a colander. Pack the blackberries in freezer containers, adding 1 part of sugar to 4 parts of black-berries. Sugar may settle to the bottom of the container. Mix thoroughly but gently after thawing if berries are to be served whole.

Mrs. Becky Cottle, Macon, Georgia

FROZEN CANTALOUPE

2 c. sugar   4 to 8 med. cantaloupes
4 c. water

Mix the sugar and water and cook until syrupy. Cool the syrup, then chill. Peel the cantaloupes and remove seed and fibers. Cut the pulp in bite-sized pieces or scoop into balls. Pack into 1-pint or 1-quart freezer cartons and shake down well. Cover with chilled syrup, leaving 1/2 to 1 inch headspace. Freeze immediately. Serve while still slightly frozen.

Mrs. Maury Hickman, Memphis, Tennessee

FROZEN BING CHERRIES

3 c. sugar   4 tsp. ascorbic acid
4 c. water   Fresh Bing cherries

Combine the sugar and water in a saucepan and bring to a boil. Simmer for 5 minutes, then cool and add the ascorbic acid. Wash and drain the cherries. Place in freezer bags or cartons. Cover with syrup and seal the bags. Freeze.

Mrs. J. F. Dunlap, El Paso, Texas

FROZEN CRANBERRIES

Firm ripe cranberries

Stem and sort the cranberries, using only tender glossy berries with a firm texture. Wash thoroughly and drain. Pack into freezer bags or containers without sugar. Seal and freeze.

Mrs. Crissie Chandler, Dundalk, Maryland

FROZEN PEACHES

1 c. orange juice	**3 c. sugar**
1 c. water	**18 peaches**

Mix the orange juice, water and sugar and stir until the sugar is dissolved. Slice the peaches and pack in freezer containers. Pour in the orange juice mixture and seal the containers. Freeze.

Mrs. Millie Lamar, Valdosta, Georgia

FRESH FROZEN PEACHES

1 tsp. ascorbic acid	**1 qt. soft ripe peaches**
1 c. (or more) sugar	

Mix the ascorbic acid and sugar. Peel and slice the peaches thin and add the sugar mixture. Let stand, stirring occasionally, until sugar is dissolved. Pack the peaches in freezer containers and seal, then freeze.

Mrs. D. D. Waldrep, Stephenville, Texas

FROZEN PINEAPPLE

2 c. sugar	**Pineapple**
1 qt. water	

Combine the sugar and water in a saucepan and bring to a boil, then cool. Pare the pineapple and remove the core and eyes. Cut in slices or cubes, as desired. Pack in freezer containers and cover with the syrup. Seal and freeze.

Aline Beasley, Austin, Texas

FREEZING FRESH STRAWBERRIES

Select firm ripe strawberries for freezing. Wash, drain and remove the hulls. Place strawberries in double-walled quilted plastic bag in portions for 1 meal. May add a cool simple sugar syrup or sugar if desired. Press all the air from unfilled portion of bag before sealing. Allow head space as foods expand when frozen. Place each bag in freezer as filled.

Photograph for this recipe on page 156.

FROZEN STRAWBERRIES

3 c. sugar
1 c. water

1 gal. fresh ripe strawberries

Mix the sugar and water in a saucepan and bring to a boil. Cool completely. Pack the strawberries carefully into plastic freezer boxes and cover with the syrup. Seal the boxes and freeze immediately. Thaw in refrigerator to serve.

Mrs. Grace Parker, Cullman, Alabama

FROZEN MELON BALLS

1 c. sugar
1 1/4 c. water

1/4 tsp. salt
1 watermelon

Mix the sugar, water and salt in a saucepan and bring to a boil, stirring to dissolve sugar. Cool the syrup and chill. Cut the watermelon in half and remove the seed. Scoop the pulp out in small balls and place in freezer containers. Pour chilled syrup over the watermelon balls and seal the containers. Freeze. Remove from freezer and refrigerate overnight for easy serving.

Mrs. Carolyn Kinney, New Orleans, Louisiana

APRICOT FREEZER JAM

2 1/2 c. ground apricots
1/8 tsp. crystalline ascorbic
   acid

2 tbsp. lemon juice
5 1/2 c. sugar
1 box powdered pectin

Mix the apricots, ascorbic acid and lemon juice, then stir in sugar. Combine the pectin and 3/4 cup water in a saucepan and bring to a boil. Boil for 1 minute, stirring constantly. Stir into fruit mixture and stir for 3 minutes. Some crystals will remain. Ladle into jars and cover at once with tight lids. Let stand at room temperature for 24 hours. Store in the freezer.

Camille Berry, Lawton, Oklahoma

UNCOOKED CRANBERRY JAM

1 lb. cranberries   1 pkg. powdered pectin
4 c. sugar   1 c. water

Put the cranberries through the fine blade of a food chopper or chop in a blender. Add enough water to make 2 cups liquid, if necessary. Combine the cranberries with sugar and let stand for 30 minutes. Stir the pectin into the water. Bring to a boil and boil rapidly for 1 minute. Remove from heat. Add the cranberry mixture and stir for 2 minutes. Pour into sterilized jelly glasses and cover. Let stand at room temperature overnight or until jelled. Seal. Store in freezer. Will keep several months in freezer.

Mrs. Elsie Sublett, Williamsburg, Kentucky

UNCOOKED PEACH JAM

3 c. crushed peaches   1 pkg. powdered pectin
5 c. sugar   1 c. water

Place the peaches in a large mixing bowl and add the sugar. Mix well and let stand for 20 minutes, stirring occasionally. Dissolve the pectin in the water and bring to a boil. Boil for 1 minute. Add the pectin solution to the peach mixture and stir for 2 minutes. Ladle into jelly glasses or freezer containers. Let stand until jam is firm. Seal and freeze.

Kathryn Lansdon, Columbia, South Carolina

NO-COOK RASPBERRY JAM

3 c. crushed raspberries   1 c. water
6 c. sugar   1 pkg. powdered pectin

Mix the raspberries and sugar well. Combine the water and pectin in a saucepan and boil for 1 minute. Mix all the ingredients, stirring for 2 minutes. Pour into desired containers. Keeps for several months in the freezer.

Rose Lawton, Wheaton, Maryland

UNCOOKED STRAWBERRY JAM

4 c. mashed strawberries   1 c. light corn syrup
Juice of 1 lemon   5 1/2 c. sugar
1 pkg. powdered pectin

Combine the strawberries and lemon juice. Sift the pectin onto the strawberries and mix, then let stand for 20 minutes. Add the syrup and sugar and mix well. Pour into jars and cover tightly. Let stand at room temperature for 24 to 48 hours or until jelled. Store in freezer. 4-5 pints.

Mrs. Marlys Cordes, Atlanta, Georgia

Frozen Baked Goods (below)

FROZEN BAKED GOODS

Breads, cakes, cookies and most kinds of pies are naturals to freeze. Cool thoroughly before wrapping. Wrap in transparent plastic film, then place in freezer. Most pies and cookies may be frozen before or after baking.

PEACH PIE FILLING FOR FREEZING

4 qt. peeled sliced peaches	10 tbsp. quick tapioca
1 tsp. ascorbic acid	1/4 c. lemon juice
1 gal. water	1 tsp. salt
3 1/2 c. sugar	

Place the peaches in a large container. Dissolve the ascorbic acid in water and pour over the peaches. Drain. Combine the peaches, sugar, tapioca, lemon juice and salt. Line four 5-inch pie pans with heavy-duty foil, extending foil 5 inches over rims. Spoon peach mixture into pans, then fold foil loosely over pans. Freeze. Remove from pans and place in plastic bags and seal. Store in freezer.

Martha Brady, Valdosta, Georgia

FROZEN PEAR PIE FILLING

3 tsp. ascorbic acid	10 tbsp. instant tapioca
1 1/2 c. sugar	4 qt. sliced pears
1 tsp. salt	1/3 c. lemon juice

Combine the ascorbic acid, sugar, salt and tapioca and sprinkle over each pear after being peeled. Add the lemon juice and mix well. Line four 8-inch pie pans with aluminum foil, freezer paper or film, extending lining 5 inches beyond rims of pans. Spoon 4 cups filling into each pan and freeze. Remove from freezer and wrap lining tightly over filling. Seal and remove from pie pans. Wrap with freezer paper and store in the freezer.

Mrs. Gwendolyn White, Eatonton, Georgia

POP-IN-PAN FROZEN STRAWBERRY PIE

4 qt. fresh strawberries	1/4 c. lemon juice
4 c. sugar	1 tsp. salt
3/4 c. instant tapioca	

Wash and hull the strawberries. Combine all ingredients and mix well. Line four 8-inch pie pans with heavy-duty foil. Let the foil extend about 6 inches beyond rims of pans. Pour in filling and fold the foil over top loosely. Freeze until firm. Remove from pans, then wrap in freezer paper and return to freezer. May be stored for 6 months. Remove foil from filling and do not thaw. Place in pastry-lined 9-inch pie pan and dot with butter. Top crust may be added. Cut slits in top crust. Bake in 425-degree oven for about 1 hour or until syrup boils with heavy bubbles that do not burst.

Mrs. Larence Potter, Rogers, Oklahoma

FREEZING BASS

1 c. salt	Bass
1 gal. ice water	

Combine the salt and ice water to make a brine. Remove the scales, entrails and fins of the bass. Cut off the heads and tails. Clean as thoroughly as for frying immediately. Soak the bass in the brine for 20 minutes, then lift out. Wrap each bass in freezer paper, then place the amount used for one meal in a moisture-vapor-proof carton and seal.

Mrs. Barbara Wallace, Natchez, Mississippi

FISH FILLETS

4 fish fillets	1 qt. water
1/4 c. salt	

Wash the fillets thoroughly. Combine the salt and water and immerse the fillets in the solution for 20 minutes, then drain. Place the fillets in a single layer on a tray or baking sheet and freeze quickly. Dip the frozen fillets in water just above freezing. A thin coating of ice will form over the fillets. Dip the fillets about 3 times for a smooth glaze. Wrap each fillet carefully in freezer paper, then place in a freezer container large enough to hold all the fillets and seal. Small fish may be glazed in this manner to prevent drying out.

Mrs. Betty Hosmer, Dothan, Alabama

Freezing Fish (below)

FREEZING FISH

Handle this perishable food quickly and carefully. Leave the small fish whole and cut the large fish into fillets. Dip lean fish in a brine solution of 1/4 cup salt to 1 quart water and fatty fish in an ascorbic acid solution of 2 tablespoons ascorbic acid to 1 quart water to help keep fish firm and reduce leakage when thawing. Wrap in transparent plastic film and seal with tape. Mark the tape with kind of dish and date. Freeze quickly.

HARD-SHELLED CRABS FOR THE FREEZER

Live hard-shelled crabs	**1 gal. water**
1/3 c. salt	

Clean the crabs. Combine the salt and water in a large kettle and bring to a boil. Drop the crabs in the boiling solution and boil for about 20 minutes. Cool thoroughly. Remove the edible meat, keeping the body and claw meat separate, if desired, for packaging. Pack in freezer cartons to within 1/2 inch of the top. Seal according to package directions and freeze. Crabs should be used within 4 months after freezing.

Mrs. Jean Wilson, Baltimore, Maryland

FROZEN OYSTERS

Fresh oysters	**1 gal. water**
1/2 c. salt	

Shuck the oysters, saving the liquor, as for immediate use. Make a brine with the salt and water, then wash the oysters in the brine. Drain well and pack in freezer containers. Seal and freeze.

Mrs. Earline Reid, Dover, Delaware

FROZEN SHRIMP

Fresh lge. shrimp	
1 c. salt	**1 gal. water**

Remove the heads and appendages of the shrimp and wash thoroughly. Combine the salt and water and wash the shrimp in the solution, then drain. Place in boiling water to cover and boil for 10 minutes. Chill in cold water, then remove the shells and sand veins. Rinse in cold water and drain. Pack in freezer containers and seal. Freeze. Cooked frozen shrimp are ready for use immediately after thawing. Use within 3 to 4 months.

Mrs. Lucy Wansley, Biloxi, Mississippi

FREEZING SHRIMP IN THE SHELL

Shrimp	**1 qt. water**
1/4 c. salt	

Wash the shrimp thoroughly. Remove the head, appendages and the vein down the back. Wash again in the salt water and drain thoroughly. Pack in freezer containers and seal, then freeze immediately. Shrimp in the shell requires more space in the freezer, but storage time is longer than for cooked shrimp.

Mrs. Fay Lowder, Winston-Salem, North Carolina

FROZEN MINCEMEAT

3 c. ground pork and beef	1 pt. cherries
2 c. raisins	3 c. sugar
1 c. vinegar	1 tsp. salt
1 c. molasses	1 tbsp. cinnamon
5 c. chopped apples	1 tbsp. nutmeg
1 No. 303 can crushed pineapple	1 tbsp. allspice

Cook the ground meat until tender, then drain, reserving 1 cup broth. Cool the broth and skim off fat. Cook the raisins in a small amount of water. Combine the meat, raisins, reserved broth, vinegar, molasses and remaining fruits in a large kettle. Mix the sugar, salt and spices and stir into meat mixture. Heat mixture to a boil, then cool. Pack in freezer containers and freeze. Gooseberries, oranges and bananas may be added, if desired. 12 pints.

Violet Roberson, Fayetteville, North Carolina

Individual Meat Loaves (below)

INDIVIDUAL MEAT LOAVES

2 lb. ground beef	1/4 tsp. pepper
1 c. evaporated milk	1/2 tsp. thyme
1 c. oatmeal	2/3 c. minced onion
2 eggs	1 tsp. Worcestershire sauce
2 tsp. salt	1/4 c. catsup
2 tsp. dry mustard	

Place the ground beef in mixing bowl, then add remaining ingredients and mix until blended. Turn into eight 3-inch cupcake cups. Bake at 350 degrees for 45 minutes. Cool and remove from cups. Wrap in transparent plastic wrap, then seal and label. Freeze. Thaw partially in refrigerator before reheating.

GROUND BEEF PATTIES

6 lb. lean ground beef

Form the ground beef into patties. Wrap each patty in aluminum foil, pressing out air. Pack in a top-opening carton. Seal according to package directions and freeze immediately. Patties may be removed as needed.

Mrs. Vera Gorham, Yuma, Arizona

SIRLOIN STEAKS

8 2-in. thick sirloin steaks

Chill the steaks in the refrigerator. Trim the fat. Place 2 pieces of freezer paper between the steaks for easy removal. Pack in a top-opening carton and seal. Freeze immediately. The steaks may be removed, one at a time or all at once, and cooked by favorite method.

Mrs. Jo Ann Langdon, Clarksdale, Mississippi

FROZEN LEG OF LAMB

1 leg of lamb

Have the butcher bone, roll and tie the leg of lamb. Chill in the refrigerator, then wrap in freezer paper and seal. Freeze. Boned lamb saves space in the freezer and provides a convenient dish for a special occasion, such as a barbecue.

Mrs. Peg Martell, Durham, North Carolina

FREEZING BROILER CHICKENS

4 broiler-chickens, dressed

Split the broilers in halves, down the back and along the breastbone. Remove the backbone. Place 2 pieces of freezer paper between the halves to separate easily, then wrap both pieces securely in freezer paper and seal. Freeze.

Mrs. Bertha Kirkland, Augusta, Georgia

FRYERS

Dressed fryers

Cut the fryers into serving pieces. Remove excess fat around the abdominal cavity and wishbone. Clean the giblets and the neck thoroughly. Wrap in freezer paper or place in freezer bags and seal. Wings, drumsticks and breasts may be wrapped together in separate packages, if desired.

Mrs. Neva Madison, Anniston, Alabama

WILD DUCKS FOR THE FREEZER

Wild ducks

Scald the ducks as soon as possible after killing. Leave the ducks in hot water until the wing and tail feathers pull out easily. Pick, clean, draw, wash and drain thoroughly as for poultry. Chill immediately. Tie the legs tightly to the breast and wrap in freezer paper. Freeze immediately. Do not freeze the giblets.

Mrs. Sara Riley, Pine Bluff, Arkansas

FREEZING EGGS

1 doz. fresh eggs **2 tsp. salt**

Wash the eggshells and break each egg into a cup. Set aside any eggs not fresh enough to be frozen and use as soon as possible. Combine the eggs in a large bowl and beat with a fork just long enough to combine. Stir in the salt and pour into freezer containers. Seal and freeze. Smaller amounts may be frozen for specific recipes.

Mrs. Mary Sawyer, Panama City, Florida

BROCCOLI

Broccoli **Water**
Salt

Wash and trim the broccoli stalks. Soak for 30 minutes in a solution of 4 teaspoons salt to 1 gallon cold water. Split lengthwise into small pieces. Heat in boiling water for 3 minutes. Remove from heat and cool in cold water, then drain. Pack the broccoli into containers, filling completely. Seal and freeze.

Alva Brooks, Bowling Green, Kentucky

BRUSSELS SPROUTS

Firm, green Brussels sprouts **1 gal. cold water**
4 tsp. salt

Remove the coarse outer leaves of the Brussels sprouts and discard imperfect sprouts. Dissolve the salt in the water and soak the Brussels sprouts for 30 minutes to remove any insects; then wash in clear water. Cook for 5 minutes in boiling water and cool in cold water, then drain. Pack the Brussels sprouts in freezer bags and seal, then freeze.

Mrs. Lorene Sinclair, Baton Rouge, Louisiana

FREEZING CORN WITH MARGARINE

2 c. fresh corn, cut from cob **1/2 stick margarine**

Combine the corn and margarine in a saucepan and cook over low heat, stirring constantly, until the corn is heated through. Cool and place in freezer bags. Seal and freeze. Use within 3 months.

Mrs. Lavoyd Russell, Marianna, Arkansas

GREEN BEANS

Tender green beans

Cut off the stem and tip ends of the beans, then cut in desired lengths. Cook in boiling water for 3 minutes, then cool quickly in ice water. Drain and pack in freezer bags or cartons and seal.

Mrs. Cindy Clay, Clarksdale, Mississippi

Freezing Casseroles (below)

FREEZING CASSEROLES

Prepare casseroles and place in freezer in oven dishes or foil pans. Wrap in transparent plastic film. Season lightly if storage is prolonged as seasoning becomes stronger. May or may not thaw before baking but if baked frozen, then must bake for longer time.

LIMA BEANS

Fresh tender lima beans

Shell and wash the lima beans and place in a large kettle. Cover with boiling water and cook for 2 minutes. Drain, reserving liquid. Remove any scum from liquid. Rinse the lima beans with ice water until cool. Pack the lima beans in freezer containers and cover with blanching liquid. Freeze.

Mrs. S. R. Singletary, Ochlochnee, Georgia

FREEZING CARROTS

Whole sm. carrots

Wash the carrots and scrape. Cook in boiling water for 5 minutes. Cool in ice water, then drain. Pack the carrots in freezer bags or cartons, alternately large and small ends to conserve space. Seal and freeze.

Mrs. Gertrude Yancey, Oklahoma City, Oklahoma

CUCUMBER SALAD

12 lge. cucumbers	1/2 c. salt
5 med. onions	2 c. sugar
1 green pepper	1 1/2 c. white vinegar
1 red pepper	

Peel and slice the cucumbers. Dice the onions and peppers or slice thin. Mix the vegetables together. Combine salt, sugar and vinegar and pour over the vegetables. Let stand for 1 hour. Pour in freezer containers and seal, then freeze.

Mrs. Jane Hawkins, Mobile, Alabama

FREEZING CORN-ON-THE-COB

Corn on cob

Boil midget corn for 7 minutes, small ears for 8 minutes and medium ears of corn for 10 minutes. Use smallest ears available for freezing on cob. Chill for 15 minutes in cold water after boiling. Drain for several minutes. Roll each ear separately in aluminum foil, then place in freezer bags and seal. Freeze. Do not thaw or remove foil to cook. Place in boiling water or bake in oven. Remove foil when ready to serve.

Mrs. Dewey Rakes, Shady Spring, West Virginia

FROZEN PARSNIPS

Parsnips

Wash the parsnips thoroughly and remove the tops. Peel and slice lengthwise in 1/4-inch strips or crosswise. Small parsnips may be cut in half. Remove core, if woody. Blanch for 3 to 4 minutes in 4 quarts boiling water per pound of parsnips. Cool and drain well. Pack in containers, then seal and freeze.

Mrs. Gay Hopkins, Beaufort, South Carolina

FREEZING SQUASH

Summer squash

Wash the squash thoroughly, then cut into 1/2-inch slices. Scald for 1 minute, then rinse with ice water until cool. Drain on paper towels. Place in a single layer on a cookie sheet and freeze. Remove when frozen. Place desired amount in plastic bags and seal. Return to freezer to store. Cookie sheet method prevents slices from sticking together.

Mrs. Lewis Truklar, Medford, Oklahoma

FROZEN OKRA

Okra	**Meal**

Wash the okra and drain well. Remove the stems and slice. Roll in meal, completely covering the okra. Place desired amount in a plastic bag and close securely with rubber band or freezer tape. Freeze. Will keep several months.

Mrs. Sam Chambers, Midland, Texas

FROZEN LOUISIANA YAM PIES

1 5-oz. package instant mashed Louisiana yams	1/2 tsp. cinnamon
	1 tsp. vanilla
1/3 c. (packed) dark brown sugar	3 eggs, separated
	1/2 c. heavy cream, whipped
1 tbsp. lemon juice	2/3 c. graham cracker crumbs
1 tsp. grated lemon peel	1 1/2 tbsp. sugar

Prepare the instant yams according to package directions, omitting the seasoning. Stir in the brown sugar, lemon juice and peel and cinnamon. Cool, then stir in the vanilla. Beat the egg yolks until thick and fluffy, then stir into the yam mixture. Beat the egg whites until stiff, but not dry. Fold into the yam mixture with the whipped cream. Combine the crumbs and sugar, then sprinkle half the crumbs in 6 individual foil tart or pie pans. Spoon in the yam mixture, then sprinkle with the remaining crumbs. Freeze until firm, then wrap in double-walled quilted plastic bags and return to freezer. Place in refrigerator for 20 to 30 minutes to mellow before serving.

Frozen Louisiana Yam Pies (above)

CHICKEN STOCK

1 4 to 5-lb. stewing chicken	1/2 tsp. whole cloves 4 peppercorns
1 1-lb. beef soupbone	2 tsp. salt
4 sm. carrots	Sprig of parsley
2 stalks of celery and leaves	1 bay leaf 2 onions

Place all the ingredients in a large kettle and add 4 quarts water. Bring to a boil, then reduce the heat. Simmer until the chicken falls from bones. Remove the chicken and set aside to use at another time. Boil the stock over high heat to reduce liquid for about 30 minutes. Strain through a sieve and cool. Skim off any fat from the top. Pour into leakproof containers and seal. Freeze immediately. Chicken stock may be used for soups, sauces, casseroles and flavor for vegetables. Add water to concentrated stock to make soups.

Mrs. Lily Manning, Birmingham, Alabama

VEGETABLE SOUP MIX

1 gal. ripe tomatoes	1 1/2 c. lima beans
6 ears of corn	2 c. okra
1 1/2 c. cream field peas	

Scald, peel and quarter tomatoes. Simmer for 2 minutes. Boil corn for 4 minutes, then cool and cut from cob. Simmer shelled peas and beans for 2 minutes. Simmer okra for 3 minutes and cool. Slice in 1-inch slices. Mix the vegetables lightly with wooden spoon. Pack in containers and seal, then freeze. 6-7 pints.

Mrs. L. L. Bagley, El Dorado, Arkansas

FROZEN MEATBALL-VEGETABLE SOUP

1 bunch carrots, diced	1 env. dry onion soup mix
1 stalk celery, diced	1 can tomatoes
3 onions, diced	3 potatoes, diced
1 lb. ground beef	

Place carrots, celery and onions in a large kettle and add 2 quarts water. Bring to a boil. Shape the beef in small balls and drop into the boiling mixture. Simmer until the meatballs are tender, then cool. Skim fat from the top and pour into leakproof containers. Seal and freeze. Empty into a large kettle and partially thaw over low heat. Add the remaining ingredients and simmer until the potatoes are tender.

Mrs. Marie Ashley, Greenville, South Carolina

FISH BROTH FOR SOUP

1 tbsp. salt	1 sm. onion, chopped
Fish heads	1/2 c. diced carrots
Fish bones	1/2 c. chopped celery
Leftover fish scraps	

Pour 2 quarts water in a kettle and add the salt. Bring to a boil, then add remaining ingredients. Simmer for 15 minutes, then allow to cool. Skim off fat and strain, reserving the broth. Pour the broth into leakproof cartons or glass jars, leaving 1 inch for expansion, then seal and freeze.

Mrs. Ada Carlson, Bay St. Louis, Mississippi

MACARONI-FISH CHOWDER

1 1-lb. package frozen cod fillets	1/2 tsp. monosodium glutamate
1/2 c. chopped celery	1/2 tsp. leaf thyme
1/4 c. chopped onion	1/2 tsp. curry powder
1/4 c. chopped parsley	1/8 tsp. pepper
1 tbsp. salad or olive oil	1/8 tsp. garlic powder
1 qt. water	2 c. elbow macaroni
2 17-oz. cans tomato juice	2 c. shredded cabbage
2 tsp. salt	1 10-oz. package frozen mixed vegetables, thawed

Partially thaw the cod, then cut into cubes. Cook the celery, onion, parsley and cod in hot oil in a large Dutch oven until vegetables are crisp-tender. Add the water, tomato juice and seasonings. Bring to a full boil, then add the macaroni gradually; add the cabbage and mixed vegetables, stirring frequently. Boil gently for 10 minutes 'or until macaroni is tender. Cool and place in plastic freezer containers. Freeze. Partially thaw before reheating to serve.

Macaroni-Fish Chowder (above)

As part of your initial preparation for the canning season, you must determine what quantities of food you should can for an adequate supply throughout the year. Since few families serve canned meat at all meals, 4 servings of canned meat a week have been allowed; in addition 10 other servings of meat, poultry, seafood or eggs are needed weekly. Adjust this guide to your family's needs and appetites. The chart that follows will help you decide what amount to preserve. Columns 1 and 2 indicate the kind of food and how often per week it is usually served; columns 4 and 5 tell you how much of this food to can in order to serve it this often. Column 3 indicates the approximate size of the serving.

FOOD PLANNING GUIDE

PRODUCT	NO. TIMES SERVED	SIZE SERVING	AMOUNT NEEDED	
			ONE PERSON	FAMILY OF 4
Citrus fruit and tomatoes (Includes juices)	7 per week— 36 weeks	1 cup	63 quarts	252 quarts
Dark Green and deep Yellow Vegetables Broccoli, spinach and other greens, carrots, pumpkin, sweet potatoes, yellow winter squash	4 per week— 36 weeks	1/2 cup	18 quarts	72 quarts
Other Fruits and Vegetables	17 per week— 36 weeks	1/2 cup	76 quarts	304 quarts
Meats, Poultry, Seafood	4 per week— 36 weeks	1/2 cup (2-3 ounces)	18 quarts or 36 pints	72 quarts or 144 pints
Soups	2 per week— 36 weeks	1 cup	18 quarts	72 quarts
Jams, Jellies, Preserves	6 per week— 52 weeks	2 tablespoons	40 half-pints	160 half-pints
Relishes	3 per week— 52 weeks	1 tablespoon	5 pints	20 pints
Pickles, Vegetable	2 per week— 52 weeks		13 pints	52 pints
Pickles, Fruit	2 per week— 52 weeks		13 quarts	52 quarts

Acid foods — foods that contain a high amount of natural acid, and foods which are preserved in vinegar. Examples are fruits, rhubarb, tomatoes, sauerkraut, pickles, and relishes.

Cap — the cover used to seal a jar. There are two kinds: (1) The two-piece metal cap that consists of a lid and screw band. The lid is fitted with a sealing compound. (2) The one-piece zinc cap that is lined with white porcelain. It is used with a rubber ring on the canning jar.

Cold or raw pack — a method of filling jars. The jars are filled with raw food, then processed in a water-bath or steam-pressure canner.

Head space — the room, from 1/4 to 1 inch, left between the food and the top of the jar after the liquid is added.

Hot pack — a method of filling jars. The jars are filled with precooked hot food, then processed in a water-bath or steam-pressure canner.

terms used

IN CANNING AND PRESERVING

Jar — a glass container made for use in home canning. There are three kinds: (1) The Mason jar that has a screw thread neck and a sloping shoulder. It seals on the top or on a sealing shoulder, depending upon the type of cap used. (2) The can or freeze jar that is a tapered, shoulderless jar that may be used for either home canning or freezing. It seals on the top with a two-piece metal cap. (3) The Lightning jar that seals with a glass lid and a rubber ring that are held in place with wires.

Lid — a round, flat cover of metal or glass used with a screw band or wire to seal a jar.

Low-acid foods — foods that contain very little natural acid. Examples are all vegetables other than rhubarb, tomatoes, and sauerkraut, and meats, poultry, seafood, and soups.

Metal band — a screw-on thread ring used with a metal or glass lid to form a two-piece metal cap.

Processing — the cooking of jars of food in a water-bath or steam-pressure canner for a long enough time to destroy microorganisms that cause spoilage.

Rubber ring — a flat rubber band that is used as a gasket between a zinc cap or a glass lid and the jar.

Spoilage — the deterioration or decay of food that makes it unfit or unsafe to consume. Indications of spoilage in canned foods include unnatural odor, uncharacteristic appearance, sourish flavor, cloudy liquid, and bulging sealing caps.

Venting or exhausting — an initial step in the steam-pressure method that permits air to escape for 10 minutes through the open vent of the canner.

The processing times listed below apply to foods canned either (1) at altitudes of less than 1000 feet above sea level for the water-bath method or (2) at altitudes of less than 2000 feet above sea level for the steam-pressure method. If you live at an altitude higher than 1000 feet above sea level and process by the water-bath method, you must make adjustments in the length of processing time. Or, if you live at an altitude higher than 2000 feet above sea level and process by the steam-pressure method, you must make adjustments in *pounds of pressure.* Both length of processing time and pounds of pressure must be increased at higher altitudes. See the ALTITUDE ADJUSTMENT GUIDE that follows the PROCESSING TIME CHART to make necessary changes if applicable.

PROCESSING TIME CHART

LOW-ACID VEGETABLES	TYPE PACK	Steam-Pressure Canner (240 degrees) 10 Pounds Pressure Processing Time in Minutes	
		1/2 PINTS AND PINTS	1 1/2 PINTS AND QUARTS
Asparagus	Raw or Hot	25	30
Beans — Green, Snap, Wax	Raw or Hot	20	25
Beans — Lima and Butter	Raw or Hot	40	50
Beets	Hot	30	35
Broccoli	Hot	30	35
Brussels Sprouts	Hot	30	35
Cabbage	Hot	30	35
Carrots	Raw or Hot	25	30
Cauliflower	Hot	30	35
Celery	Hot	30	35
Corn, Whole-kernel	Raw or Hot	55	85
Corn, Cream-style	Hot	85	Not recommended
Eggplant	Hot	30	40
Greens (all kinds)	Hot	70	90
Hominy	Hot	60	70
Mixed Vegetables	Hot	Length of time needed for vegetable requiring longest processing time	
Mushrooms	Hot	30	Not recommended
Okra	Hot	25	40
Parsnips	Hot	30	35
Peas — Blackeye, Crowder, Field	Raw or Hot	35	40
Peas — Green or "English"	Raw or Hot	40	40
Peppers, Green	Hot	35	Not recommended
Pimentos	See Acid Vegetables		
Potatoes, White	Hot	30	40

PROCESSING TIME CHART

Steam-Pressure Canner (240 degrees)
10 Pounds Pressure
Processing Time in Minutes

LOW-ACID VEGETABLES	TYPE PACK	1/2 PINTS AND PINTS	1 1/2 PINTS AND QUARTS
Potatoes, Sweet	Hot and Dry	65	95
Potatoes, Sweet	Hot and Wet	55	90
Pumpkin	Hot	65	80
Rutabagas	Hot	30	35
Salsify or Oyster Plant	Hot	25	35
Spinach	Hot	70	90
Squash, Summer	Hot	30	40
Squash, Winter	Hot	65	80
Tomatoes	See Acid Vegetables		
Turnips	Hot	30	35
MEATS, POULTRY, SEAFOODS			
Chili	Hot	75	90
Chopped Meat — Beef, Veal, Lamb, Mutton, Pork, Chevron, Venison	Hot	75	90
Corned Beef	Hot	75	90
Cracklings and Ham	Raw	50	60
Goulash, Meat Sauce, Stew	Hot	60	75
Headcheese, Pork Sausage	Hot	75	90
Pork Tenderloin	Hot or Raw	75	90
Roasts — Beef, Veal, Lamb, Mutton, Pork, Chevron, Venison	Hot	75	90
Spareribs	Hot	75	90
Steaks and Chops — Beef, Veal, Lamb, Mutton, Pork, Chevron, Venison	Hot or Raw	75	90
Poultry, Rabbit and Squirrel — Boned	Hot	75	90
On Bone	Hot or Raw	65	75
Chicken a la King	Hot	65	75
Roast Poultry	Hot	65	75
Clams		70	Not recommended
Crab Meat		100 at 5 lbs.	Not recommended
Mackerel, Trout, Salmon, Shad, etc.		100	Not recommended
Shrimp		45	Not recommended
Smelt (in Tomato Sauce)		50	60
Tuna		90	Not recommended
SOUPS			
Bean and Split Pea	Hot	50	60
Chicken	Hot	30	45

PROCESSING TIME CHART

LOW-ACID VEGETABLES	TYPE PACK	Steam-Pressure Canner (240 degrees) 10 Pounds Pressure Processing Time in Minutes	
		1/2 PINTS AND PINTS	1 1/2 PINTS AND QUARTS
Clam Chowder and Fish Chowder	Hot	100	Not recommended
Tomato	Hot	20	30
Vegetable	Hot	Length of time needed for vegetable requiring longest processing time	

FRUITS	TYPE PACK	Water-bath (212 degrees) Processing Time in Minutes		
		1/2 PINTS	PINTS	1 1/2 PINTS AND QUARTS
Apples	Hot	15	15	20
Applesauce	Hot	10	10	10
Apricots	Raw	25	25	30
Apricots	Hot	20	20	25
Berries	Raw	10	10	15
Berries	Hot	10	10	15
Cherries	Raw	20	20	25
Cherries	Hot	10	10	15
Currants	See Berries			
Figs	Hot	20	25	30
Grapes, Ripe	Raw	15	15	20
Grapes, Unripe	Raw	20	20	25
Grapefruit	Raw	10	10	10
Guavas	Hot	15	15	20
Loquats	Hot	15	15	20
Mixed Fruits	Hot	20	20	25
Nectarines	See Apricots			
Peaches	Raw	25	25	30
Peaches	Hot	20	20	25
Pears	Hot	20	20	25
Persimmons	Hot	15	15	20
Pineapple	Hot	15	15	20
Plums	Hot	20	20	25
FRUIT JUICES	Hot	See individual recipes, for processing temperatures vary according to fruit used.		

ACID VEGETABLES

Pimentos	Hot	40	40	45
Rhubarb	Hot	10	10	10
Sauerkraut	Raw	30	30	30
Tomatoes	Raw	35	35	45
Tomatoes	Hot	10	10	15
Tomato Juice	Hot	10	10	15

The following chart lists some common problems that often occur in home canning and preserving, their probable causes, and suggested remedies. When the problem may indicate spoilage, it is noted as such in the first column. You should be especially aware of signs of spoilage — *spoiled foods should not be served.* Look for these indications of spoilage each time you open a jar of home-canned food: leaking jars; bulging caps; spurting liquid and gas bubbles; cloudy liquid; sediment in the liquid; unnatural food odor or appearance; soft, mushy, slippery, or moldy food. Spoilage is often caused by defective jars and seals, incorrect procedure, underprocessing of food, or improper storage conditions.

common
problems
IN CANNING AND PRESERVING

PROBLEM (Product Usable Unless Spoilage Is Indicated)	CAUSE	PREVENTION
Fruits darken after they have been removed from jar.	Fruits have not been processed long enough to destroy enzymes.	Process each fruit by recommended method and for recommended length of time. Time is counted when water reaches a full boil in the canner.
Pink, red, blue, or purple color in canned apples, pears, peaches, and quinces.	A natural chemical change that occurs in cooking the fruit.	None
Green vegetables lose their bright green color.	Heat breaks down chlorophyll, the green coloring matter in plants.	None
Green vegetables turn brown.	1. Vegetables were overcooked. 2. Vegetables were too mature for canning.	1. Time precooking and processing exactly. 2. Asparagus tips should be tight and the entire green

PROBLEM*	CAUSE	PREVENTION
(*Product Usable Unless Spoilage Is Indicated)		
	3. Vegetables not covered with liquid.	portion tender. Pods of green beans should be crisp and meaty and the beans tiny. Peas, Lima beans, and all other beans and peas which are shelled should be green.
		3. Make sure vegetables are covered sufficiently with water.
White crystals on canned spinach.	Calcium and oxalic acid in spinach combine to form harmless calcium oxalate.	None
White sediment in bottom of jars of vegetables. May denote spoilage.	1. Starch from the food. 2. Minerals in water used. 3. Bacterial spoilage . . . liquid is usually murky, food soft. (Do not use.)	1. None 2. Use soft water. 3. Process each food by recommended method and for recommended length of time.
Cloudy liquids. May denote spoilage.	1. Spoilage. (Do not use.) 2. Minerals in water. 3. Starch in vegetable.	1. Process each food by recommended method and for recommended length of time. 2. Use soft water. 3. None
Jar seals, then comes open. Spoilage evident. Do not use.	1. Food spoilage from underprocessing. 2. Disintegration of particles of food left on the sealing surface. 3. Hairlike crack in the jar.	1. Process each food by recommended method and for recommended length of time. 2. Wipe sealing surface and threads of jar with clean, damp cloth before capping. 3. Check jars; discard ones unsuitable for canning.
Zinc caps bulge. May denote spoilage.	1. Cap screwed too tight before processing. (Condition is evident as jar is removed from canner.) 2. Food spoils from underprocessing. (Condition evident after jar has cooled and has been stored from a day to a few months.) Do not use.	1. Screw cap tight, then loosen about 1/4 inch before putting jar in canner. 2. Process each food by recommended method and for recommended length of time.

PROBLEM* (*Product Usable Unless Spoilage Is Indicated)	CAUSE	PREVENTION
Black spots on underside of metal lid.	Natural compounds in some foods cause a brown or black deposit on the underside of the lid. This deposit is harmless and does not mean the food is unsafe to eat.	None
Soft or slippery. pickles. Spoilage evident. Do not use.	1. Brine or vinegar used was too weak. 2. Pickles were not kept covered with liquid. 3. Scum was not kept removed from top of brine. 4. Pickles were not heated long enough to destroy spoilage microorganisms. 5. Jars were not sealed air-tight while boiling hot. 6. Pickles were not processed in water-bath canner.	1. Use pure refined salt. Use vinegar of 4-6 percent acidity. Use a recipe for modern day use. 2. Pickles should be covered with liquid at all times, during the brining process and when in the jar. 3. Scum should be removed daily during the brining process. 4. Follow recommended method of processing for recommended length of time. 5. Each jar should be filled boiling hot and band tightened immediately before filling next jar. Pickles should be kept boiling hot throughout packing process. 6. Process for 10 minutes.
Shriveled pickles.	Too much salt, sugar, or vinegar was added to the cucumbers at one time.	Start with a weaker solution, of brine, sugar, or vinegar and gradually add the full amount called for in recipe. Use recipe developed for modern day use.
White sediment in bottom of jars of firm pickles.	Harmless yeasts have grown on the surface and then settled.	None. The presence of a small amount of the white sediment is normal.
Jelly is cloudy.	1. Fruit used was too green. 2. Fruit may have been cooked too long before straining. 3. Juice may have been squeezed from fruit.	1. Fruit should be firm-ripe. 2. Fruit should be cooked only until it is tender. 3. To obtain the clearest jelly possible, let juice drip through cotton flannel bag.

PROBLEM (Product Usable Unless Spoilage Is Indicated)	CAUSE	PREVENTION
	4. Jelly poured into jars too slowly. 5. Jelly mixture was allowed to stand before it was poured into the jars.	4. Next time, work more quickly. 5. Immediately upon reaching jellying point, pour into jars and seal.
Jelly contains glass-like particles.	1. The mixture may have been cooked too little. 2. The mixture may have been cooked too slowly or too long. 3. Undissolved sugar, which was sticking to the pan, washed into the jelly as it was poured.	1. Too short a cooking period results in the sugar not dissolving completely and not mixing thoroughly with the fruit juice. 2. Long, slow cooking results in too much evaporation of the water content of the fruit. 3. Ladle juice into jars instead of pouring it. Or, carefully wipe side of pan free of sugar crystals with a damp cloth before filling jars.
Bubbles are in jelly. May denote spoilage.	1. If bubbles are moving, jelly is spoiling; usually the air-tight seal has been broken. (Do not use.) 2. If bubbles are standing still, utensil from which jelly was poured was not held close to top of jar or jelly was poured slowly and air was trapped in the hot jelly.	1. Use vacuum sealing next time. Be sure to test for seal before storing jars. 2. Hold utensil close to top of jar and pour into jar quickly.
Jelly "weeps".	1. "Weeping" usually occurs in quick-setting jellies and is due to the quantity of acid and the quality of pectin in the fruit. 2. Storage conditions were not ideal.	1. None 2. Store in cool, dark, and dry place.
Jelly ferments. Spoilage evident. Do not use. Jelly molds.	Yeasts grow on jelly when seal is not airtight (usually noticeable on jars sealed with paraffin) causing the jelly to break through paraffin and weep.	Use vacuum sealing next time. Test for seal before storing jelly.
May denote spoilage; do not use.	Jar was not sealed properly, allowing mold to grow on surface of jelly.	Use vacuum sealing next time. Test for seal before storing jelly.

SEASONINGS GUIDE

SPICES	FLAVOR	USES	
		WHOLE	**GROUND**
Allspice	Blend of nutmeg, clove, cinnamon	Jams, jellies, fruit and vegetable pickles, vegetable relishes, tomato catsup, and sauce, fruit sauces, fish	Butters, jams, preserves, chutneys, fruit sauces, meat sauces, tomato juice, mincemeat
Chilies	Hot, pungent	Tomato sauce, vegetable pickles	
Cinnamon	Sweet, pungent	Jams, jellies, fruit and vegetable pickles, vegetable relishes, tomato catsup, fruit sauces	Butters, jams, conserves, chutneys, fruit sauces, mincemeat, vegetable relishes, fruits
Cloves	Strong, sweet, pungent	Jams, jellies, fruit and vegetable pickles, vegetable relishes, tomato sauce, fruit sauces, meats, fish	Butters, jams, preserves, mincemeat, vegetable relishes, tomato juice
Ginger	Spicy, sweet, pungent	Jellies, preserves, fruit and vegetable pickles	Butters, jams, conserves, preserves, honeys, chutneys, fruit sauces, meat sauces, mincemeat, vegetable relishes, fruits
Mace	Similar to nutmeg		Butters, jams, conserves
Nutmeg	Sweet, warm, spicy undertone	Jellies, vegetable pickles	Butters, conserves, jams, preserves, mincemeat, fruits
Paprika	Slightly sweet		Tomato catsup, chili sauce, goulash
Pepper, Black	Hot, biting, pungent	Corned beef, chicken soup, vegetable pickles	Meat sauces, tomato puree, pork sausage
Pepper, Red	Hot, pungent	Vegetable pickles, vegetable relishes, chili sauce, chutneys, fruit sauces, soups	
Turmeric			Vegetable pickles, vegetable relishes, chutneys

HERBS	FLAVOR	USES
Basil	Sweet, warm, pungent undertone	Tomatoes, tomato paste
Bay Leaves	Pungent	Tomato paste, sauce, juice; vegetable pickles; meat; fish; poultry
Marjoram	Aromatic, bitter undertone	Tomato sauce, meat sauces
Oregano	Strong, aromatic, bitter undertone	Tomato paste, meat sauces
Tarragon	Similar to anise	Vegetable pickles

SEEDS	FLAVOR	USES
Anise	Licorice	Fruit and vegetable pickles
Caraway	Slightly sharp, sweet undertone	Vegetable pickles, sauerkraut
Cardamom	Aromatic, pungent	Vegetable pickles
Celery	Warm, slightly bitter	Vegetable pickles, vegetable relishes, tomato catchup, chili sauce
Dill	Faint caraway tang	Vegetable pickles
Mustard	Sharp, hot pungent	Vegetable pickles, vegetable relishes, chutneys, tomato catsup

ALTITUDE ADJUSTMENT GUIDE

WATER-BATH METHOD	Increase processing time if the time called for is:		STEAM-PRESSURE METHOD	
Altitude	20 Minutes or Less	More than 20 Minutes	Altitude	Process at pressure of:
1,000 feet	1 minute	2 minutes	2,000- 3,000 feet	11 1/2 pounds
2,000 feet	2 minutes	4 minutes	3,000- 4,000 feet	12 pounds
3,000 feet	3 minutes	6 minutes	4,000- 5,000 feet	12 1/2 pounds
4,000 feet	4 minutes	8 minutes	5,000- 6,000 feet	13 pounds
5,000 feet	5 minutes	10 minutes	6,000- 7,000 feet	13 1/2 pounds
6,000 feet	6 minutes	12 minutes	7,000- 8,000 feet	14 pounds
7,000 feet	7 minutes	14 minutes	8,000- 9,000 feet	14 1/2 pounds
8,000 feet	8 minutes	16 minutes	9,000-10,000 feet	15 pounds
9,000 feet	9 minutes	18 minutes		
10,000 feet	10 minutes	20 minutes		

INDEX

190

191

PHOTOGRAPHY CREDITS: Ball Corporation; Sugar Information, Inc.; The American Spice Trade Association; General Foods Kitchens; United Fresh Fruit and Vegetable Association; Processed Apples Institute; Florida Citrus Commission; McIlhenny Company; California Dried Fig Advisory Board; Standard Fruit Steamship Company: Cabana Bananas; Apple Pantry: Washington State Apple Commission; National Kraut Packers Association; California Strawberry Advisory Board; Louisiana Yam Commission; National Macaroni Institute; Nabisco, Inc.; Saran Wrap.

Printed in the United States of America.